KALEIDOSCOPE:
My Changing World

For
vivian & Dan
with many happy memories

Love,
Grace

Grace Harlow Klein

Grace Harlow Press

Other titles by Grace Harlow Klein:
Remembering Junie
A Bridge of Returning:
An Empowering Journey
Loss: A Personal Journey of Empowerment
Transition: The Space Between

Available here:
www.graceharlowklein.com/store/

ISBN: 978-0-9800035-3-6

Contact: www.graceharlowklein.com
        grace@graceharlowklein.com

For Armin

It was twenty nine and a half years we had together, before death took Armin in a devastating and painful to watch process of robbing him of his life. Yet his warmth and smile and connecting eyes remained until three days before he closed them and allowed death to come. I am incredibly grateful to Peter who helped me care for him at home and that Armin always knew I was there. In the end, it seemed that I was all he needed.

Every day we had together was a day of growth
  —of love that endured all kinds of challenges
  —of connection we had neither known
    before
  —of conflicts in two people coming from
    different worlds
  —of tenderness that was there from the
    beginning and remained
  —of intimacy—so that I could say with
    confidence,
  I knew him more than anyone,
even though I did not meet him until he was 54.
  In the same way, I felt known by him—
as I had not been known before.

As it became clear what was happening, I turned to our dear friend, and Armin's first piano teacher, Vivian Weilerstein, whose music, with Don, had been so much a part of our life.

The concert played by Vivian and Don and Alisa Weilerstein, in the beautiful Kilbourn Hall of the Eastman School of Music, became the centerpiece of an 80th birthday celebration of his 58 years as a psychotherapist in the person-centered tradition. I wanted all those he had touched and those who meant so much to him to be able to tell him what he meant to them. He said, afterwards, "I know that I am loved and my life has been worthwhile." That was what I wanted him to know, this proud but unassuming man.

I miss him incredibly. He is still a vital presence in my and our continued life journey.

ARMIN IN PARIS

VIVIAN, ALISA, AND DON WEILERSTEIN

v

And for Enduring Friendship

CERALD BAUMAN

VIRGINIA WHITMIRE

VIII

Acknowledgments

I am most grateful to Robyn York whose skill in artistic book design has shaped my work over the past years. She is a joy to work with, her presence and magnetism an addition to my life and our friendship. I am happy for her in the new directions in her life.

For reading my manuscripts and providing valuable feedback, I am grateful to my sister, Coralie Harlow Robertson. I take great pleasure in seeing her book take form on living after loss.

I am grateful to my friends who helped me when I asked. Their vision for my work gave the book the title and inspired the poem, "Kaleidoscope." Thank you Chris, Rebecca, Denise, Peter, Jackie and Vu for your support, understanding and respect for my work—and for our friendship.

My friend Pat Ward-Baker is both friend and a great support in that we as "older" women are creating new visions for our work.

The gardens throughout my books are the result of a special partnership and friendship with Milli Picconi, owner of Perennial Designs. She appeared at my door at just the right moment—and never left!

To Julia Cameron whose Morning Pages writing kept me "sane" through difficult times. I discovered her book at the beginning and still write them!

Preface

When I resigned from my university administrative position in 1997, I had a year's sabbatical before I returned to teaching, a right guaranteed by my position as a tenured professor. During that year I began to write prose poetry, to take classes in painting and in photography, an avocation I had enjoyed during vacations for many years. The writing of poetry was new for me, but it seemed natural in my home where my husband, Armin, had written poems for much of his adult life. Painting was only a whisper in the back of my mind, that I would like to try it to see if it was something I would enjoy. I had lived in my condo near the university for several years during the weeks of my work. An artist and I became acquainted and I enjoyed going to see his work. My efforts to talk with him about his work were not successful, however, as my world of feelings had no relevance for how he thought about his art. But it was a new world opening for me to express my feelings and experiences of loss following the deaths of my mother that same fall and of my father five years earlier.

When I returned to the university I taught a course on Death, Loss and Transition. It is hard to say at this point the impact of the course on my poetry, but it is unmistakably there as I began to write about the deaths of my mother, father and youngest sister.

Over three years later, and with the help of my attorney, I proposed to the university a buy-out of my tenure which was eventually agreed to. The poetry in this collection includes those events, but focuses on a more positive optimistic future, despite the diagnosis of prostate cancer in my husband which I wrote about in an, as yet, unfinished manuscript, Life's Unexpected Lessons.

The first two collections of the poems written during those years were published in 2010, thirteen years after the beginning of the events: A Bridge of Returnng: An Empowering Journey and Loss: A Personal Journey of Empowerment. They were preceded in 2007 by a short book, Remembering Junie, our amazing yellow Labrador. All of the books combine my prose poetry, art and photography.

I continued to work on the next book, Transition: The Space Between (2015) but stopped in the final illness and death of my husband in November, 2011 as the experiences of death and loss continued. While the majority of the poems were written in that early period, spanning 1997–2001, recording very present and powerful feelings and experiences, each of the books has been influenced by the passage of time and what actually happened in my life as it moved forward. As such, they reflect the accuracy of experience and outlook as I lived them and the realities of my life which followed. These realities make it clear that we are not in control of the events in our lives—but only how we choose to live them.

In 2012, I returned to Provence, a place which we greatly enjoyed and were very happy together, for a working vacation—
—to continue my healing
     from the devastating loss of Armin
—to finish <u>Change</u>—*as I thought of it then*
—to begin to write our love story
—to give me time and space alone and away
     to think about the next chapter of my life
     alone, without Armin in my daily world.

I was once again in that space between—lost between a known world of belonging and love, despite Armin's devastating illnesses, and an unknown world ahead which must be created, not unlike those experiences in my poetry. Events in my practice as a psychotherapist once more put the completion of my book on hold until I was able to finish <u>Transition: The Space Between</u> at the end of 2015.

As I work on the completion of this manuscript, I see the process I was in all of those years ago, of exploring new avenues of creativity, but also reflecting about my life with Armin. It is a similar process to the now of my learning to live again without Armin here, alternating between deep sadness in the loss of him with joy and gratefulness in the richness of the life we shared.

It is not clear where this path will take me—beyond finishing this book!

I hope my experiences touch the reader's life, providing validity to their own experiences and support for the importance of their voices to speak for each of them.

Photography credits:

I am grateful to:
Charles Ball for the beautiful wedding photographs which preserve the memories of that special day. I am deeply touched by the beauty and intimacy he recorded in that wonderful day. And for the 20th anniversary photographs which he also took.

James Schuck for the beautiful family photographs from the 80th birthday celebration for Armin.

The remaining photographs are credited, those of the author or are unknown from family archives,

I am deeply touched by the power of photographs and of Armin's poetry which preserve images and thoughts and feelings which would otherwise be lost to memory. Recently, in retrieving old childhood family photographs for my brother, I am filled with gratefulness to my mother who began this tradition of family photographs at the very beginning of my life.

Contents

Prose Poetry

Adventure

I have lived many lifetimes—
      Daughter, mother, lover, wife
Young, naïve, excited about life
      Battle-scarred veteran
Learning from all my adventures
      Always looking for more.

Now I am on a new adventure
      Creating a new life for myself—
Dreaming new dreams, letting go of the old
      That bound me in time and space.
They limited me as surely as those women
      Whose feet were bound in long ago China
To make them more desirable—
      While making it impossible for them to walk.

Maybe that was really the hidden point.

Being Different

I have struggled my whole life with being different,
    Different from others in my family,
But also in my group of friends growing up
    And in the worlds of my work
And of my relationships.

Sometimes my differentness felt like being special
    As I experienced with my grandfather
When I was young and first.
    In those times I soar
Knowing that I am fortunate—
    To have the unique gifts of ability
And sensitivity with which I was endowed.
    "Good genes," our father told us.

Other times I realize with amazement
    That I am interested in different things.
It is as if I come from a different planet
    And see and hear different visions and voices
Than those of others around me.

One day I realized I like older people.
    I like the richness of their life experiences.
I feel comfortable with their maturity
    And have sought out
These very special people to be a part of my life.
    Now, I am one of them!

I have been fascinated and touched by feelings
       Which are often hidden from the surface
Of the world in which we live.
       I find great joy
In connecting with those feelings—
       My own and those of others
              Which enrich my life.

But other times my feelings of differentness
       Bring excruciating pain
Brought on by my own sense of differentness
       From others
              Or exclusion by others
                     From being a part of belonging.
In those times I feel like an outsider,
       A two-headed monster in my own family
I once said.
       In those times my heart aches,
My body in pain,
       The essential part of me that makes me, me
Cast aside, judged as unworthy.
       But I also find myself judging others
In relationship to me
       Defining my Self as different,
Not wanting to be a part of a group
       That I find boring or uninteresting.

Perhaps the hardest experiences have been those
       In which I choose you,
But you do not choose me—

Despite my knowing
     I am important to you.

In those times my sense of uniqueness
     Sustains me and I realize it is your loss
And I learn and gain
     While going on to find
My own shared sense of belonging,
     Celebrating my differentness.

When I first came to Rochester, the Rose of Sharon
bush was blooming by the church at the corner.
Armin picked a blossom for me—as he often did in
the years afterwards. Now I have my own bush
in my garden and memories of him.

The Yearning

In my cleaning I found a long lost friend today
 As well as old reminders of the world I left—
  Leaving me feeling sad.

Three years ago
 I went to Julia Cameron's workshop,
By then I had already been writing
 Morning Pages,
Having discovered her Artist's Way.
 I have filled several books
Of my early morning musings
 Which have kept me sane
Through this difficult time of exploring my world.

I met Tim Wheater's music on the way.
 And then he was there!
I listened to him in the workshop
 Play the haunting sounds of his flute
  And his equally haunting music of
  The Yearning.

The story of the music is as interesting
 As the music is penetrating.
As I listened then, I wrote with tears
 Streaming down my face.
And now the music reaches in
 And touches once again.
The sadness I still run away from

But yet allow myself to feel
      In moments such as these.

We were asked to write a letter
      To the God of Creativity
Or for me, the Spirit of the Universe.
      My heart opened to the process
Of feeling grateful for the life I've lived.

I bought The Yearning to take home with me
      As I returned to a world of work
In which I did not belong,
      Yet still needed to be in.
I listened to the music coming and going
      And sometimes in between.

My anxiety was often so high
      I could scarcely breathe.
The listening and flowing with the sounds
      Of yearning to be anywhere
But where I was,
      My mind stilled, my breathing deepened.
I could face the next hour,
      The challenges of being in that space
Where I no longer wanted to be.

For all that year of school
      Fall, Winter, and Spring
I listened and breathed my way through.
      And then, in one fit of cleaning my car,
I lost the tape.

Though I looked high and low it did not reappear
    And I realized I was surviving
On my own
    Without the breathless anxiety I had known.

Hearing it again, I feel the sadness
    But purer now—for me alone
Separated from the anxiety and fear.

I feel the yearning for a world
    Once filled with promise—
        But is no longer.

Now I face the future
    To find my new yearnings
        Of work and beauty and love
        And belonging.

Intimacy

This business of intimacy
    Is a confusing labyrinth
As old hurts emerge
    In tender moments of vulnerability,
Surprising and confusing to us both.

I often imagine that life can be tranquil
    That we will finally reach a place
Of mutual understanding and love
    That transcends time and separateness.

I wonder when I hear people say,
    "We never fight or have real disagreements."
What magical land do they inhabit
    That seems so far removed
From my own persistent struggles?

Then I turn it all inward and attack myself.
    What deficiency do I bring to all of this
That makes it so impossible
    To achieve that place of tranquility
I so desire.

Yet in my saner moments
    I realize that all this I bring
Is the result of a life lived fully.
    Never content with the present,
Always wanting to explore further
    This unknown land of intimacy.

I content myself with the notion of growth,
    That each new hump in the road
Brings old lives together with the present
    In this complex and beautiful world
Of knowing another—
    This shared world of intimacy.

21

Preservation

"Creativity occurs in the moment," Julia wrote
    In <u>The Artist's Way</u>.
And in this moment I am sad.
    I am trapped in a vise between my self
And others who are offended by the changes
    I have made to my house.
They have refused to allow me to have skylights
    For my studio,
Saying it destroys the character of the old house
    Which stands in a preservation district.
I am told they would fine us and take our home
    If we refuse to comply.

The strength of those controls overpowers me.
    I want to fight but I am deeply hurt
That something so important to me
    Could produce such anger in others.

The larger issues pour in like a flood,
    Magnifying the kind of society we live in
Where people are so willing to override
    The wishes of others
Even in the privacy of our own home.

I know to others this is not a serious issue.
    I even try to prepare myself
That I can live without the skylights
    And find other ways to bring the light
Into my life, if not my studio.

How much of their anger
>Is because we broke the rule
Defying their importance in the scheme of things?

Or is it how strong they feel the damage is
>Of putting skylights in an old house,
No matter how dark it is?
>I don't know.
It is another door closing
>Like so many I have felt
And all I can do is weep
>Letting the tears wash away the pain
Until there is quietness inside of me.

* * * * * * * *

Postscript: I am not fond of "preservation!"
>Eventually, with an attorney, we were allowed
to keep two of the largest of the five skylights. We
offered to give up two, but still they had to extract
their pound of flesh, not approving the one for
the bathroom. I became a skylight hunter in
the process, finding many in our neighborhood,
including one in our own home! And in the grey of
Rochester winters, I can't imagine why they do not
promote the use of them! But the greatest irony was
seeing a whole row of skylights along the Right Bank
in Paris in buildings that go back hundreds of years!

At the Beach

Sitting at the beach, often my favorite place to be,
     I am restless.
In the exotic place of Borneo,
     Far removed from my usual life,
I have come with my special person, Jean,
     To this land of Orangutans
That she wanted to see.

She is Jean, married to my grandfather
     When I was five.
She was 29; he 65, an unlikely pair.
     But special to all of us
In the gifts she brought to our world.
     We have a long and complicated history,
But in this tale, I was visiting her
     In Colorado Springs
Where she lives in a retirement community.

She kept talking about the orangutans,
     Having traveled the world
With friends who now are dead
     Or too frail to travel.
I realized I could take her
     In this new freedom I have.
At 87, her last hurrah she called it.

I keep wondering what my life is about
     Or supposed to be about
As if there is some purpose to discover

Or some meaning to create
      Beyond the moment.

In this new world I am evolving
      I know I am privileged beyond measure,
Despite the losses of meaning and peacefulness.
      But I cannot yet feel a coherence
Of people, places and things
      Which would occupy my energy
And give meaning to my life.

The farther I travel,
      The more I see myself in a larger context
Of people struggling merely for existence.
      They sell their wares here in the marketplace
To keep food on the table
      And clothes on their backs.
While I am privileged to travel
      And leave behind my resources
As a small token in their changing economy.

I look at others far more privileged than I
      In the world of material goods
But I see no place
      Where I could even envy their way of life
Or imagine its contributing
      To this search for meaning in mine.

I come back to this world of relationships
      That one human being can give to another

The gifts of presence, caring and connection
    In these fleeting moments
We share upon this earth.

From my own pain and search
    I realize that I have gifts to share
About how each of us makes meaning in our lives,
    And struggles
To find both peace and happiness
    Through the pain of loss, and the loneliness
Of missed connection—
    Even with those with whom
We expect to be most close.

This world of caring and intimacy
    Is a brave new world.
It is made possible only by the vision
    Of people learning to love and share
Their most personal and deepest
    Hopes and dreams for themselves
With those they love.

Somewhere in all of that
    Is my place,
If only I can find it.

The Beach Again

I have escaped my usual world.
      Freedom provided the opportunity
To take my friend to Borneo,
      Pursuing her latest adventure
As she influenced my world so long ago.
      I have made it possible for her
To fulfill this dream at eighty-seven.

We have each broken free
      Of the confines of home and routine
And sit now on a tropical beach
      On the other side of the world.
The heat of the sun
      Is shaded by our big umbrella,
But still the sun makes my mind lazy
      While the images of this world
Raise all kinds of questions for me of mine.

The old and new are everywhere.
      This tropical beach resort is new,
A world of luxury and relaxation.
      The people are friendly
And welcome us to visit
      And learn about their world.

Old primitive houses sit beside new modern ones
      The glare of night time television
Catches my eye repeatedly
      As we journey one evening.

The rice is grown in this region
> In ways old and new,
Cut by hand side by side with the machine
> Moving through the wet fields
On caterpillar treads.
> The Upper Montane forest
Is too high for rice to grow
> But the vegetables grown
On mountain hillsides are brighter and greener
> Growing so close to the sun.

The university has opened in this country
> But compulsory education for young children
Is still not possible
> In the remote areas of the mountains.
The children are needed to help in the farming
> And there are no teachers
Or roads to reach them.
> All of this is there in the Sunday market
Where the local people bring their wares—
> Fish and vegetables, pineapples
And things I don't even recognize.
> (But to my dismay, I do recognize
The Kentucky Fried Chicken sign
> In the shop right next to the market!)

The sights and smells call my world into question.
> Who am I,
One in this overwhelming world
> Of change and not change?

What is it that I bring
　　　To contribute to this human kind?
The wealth of my world is modest
　　　Among the wealthy
But so far beyond so many.
　　　I feel humbled by it all.

Everywhere here I hear the sounds of progress—
　　　Of a country and people reaching
For their own dreams.
　　　They search for their place in the good life,
Beyond the colonial days of yesteryear,
　　　Afraid of losing what was strong
While embracing the new.

And I? What do I preserve of the old,
　　　This journey with its childhood connection
To a woman who first made my world larger
　　　By her sense of travel and adventure.

What, if any, of the roads I have traveled, can I share
　　　With others, this connection with past
And present and future
　　　That might encourage their dreams?

* * * * * * * *

Postscript: This trip to Borneo became a yearly adventure in which I took Jean someplace she wanted to go, none as exotic as Borneo, but the Evangeline country in Louisiana, Estes Park in Colorado and in the last two years only the 60 miles to Walmart or 30 to the Chinese restaurant she still enjoyed.

I learned to listen to her and became aware that she saved her internal world for me to hear her worries, often about her health. I would listen closely and then say, "You're not dying yet!" which was very reassuring to her. We talked of the ending of life and I gave her tools she could use to stay in control of herself which eased her fears of dependency and loss of faculties— this independent woman who had dreamed of Alaska from her childhood home in Oklahoma and then went to live there. She was an English teacher and then had amazing adventures going to the Eskimo villages to help with learning and later building a cabin on Lynn Canal, walking the half mile or so to it.

On her 97th birthday, she spoke with me by phone with great animation about her day—who got the special rum cake made by her friend, Colleen, who the regular cake. She was thrilled with the flowers I had sent, and said that the dozen roses were the first she had ever received! I was glad to be the sender for my sisters, brother and me and very touched by the email she sent which I keep, her validation of me— to me.

Twelve days later, when I called, she was dying. I asked the nurse what happened and she said that ever since her birthday, Jean had said that she was finished. Using what I had given her, perhaps, she empowered herself in this final act of independence. The next morning she was gone—on the same day they were to dismantle her apartment in independent living.

I wrote a Blog, "Remembering Jean Harlow." Some of her former students wrote to add to it, the most touching from the men who, knowing how demanding she was as a teacher, did Not take her class and realized later how much they had missed.

I miss her too, this woman from my childhood who brought a much larger world to me—her sense of adventure, making my world larger in the gifts she gave me—the first, a silver ring from Mexico and postcards of the Shrine of Guadaloupe in Mexico City. I wore the ring to school and, when asked, lent it to a classmate—who "lost" it, learning a painful lesson in third grade! The maple leaf pin from Canada, I still have!

Her relationship with my grandfather, whom I adored, the uniqueness of their match, she young, he old, she tall and statuesque, he short with his cowboy boots and Stetson hat—quite a pair they made!

Her world of education, she an English teacher with a master's degree, somehow influenced the possibility in my mind.

My sister gave me a letter found in my mother's belongings after her death. I had written a letter to my grandmother telling her about the weekend I spent alone with Jean—such a treat both to be away from my noisy home of children—and with her!

I am grateful for the place she had in my life, for the reconnection we made after a break of many years, of learning that she loved me—despite her absence— of visiting her alone in Alaska— and again with Armin, of her return to my family for my father's birthday after an absence of forty years, of learning that misunderstanding can be clarified, old wounds healed.

Over the years she gave me many gifts of her Alaska world which I treasure in my home. And then the boxes came—the photograph I had given her of Chico, the squirrel who visited her each year at her cabin, her degrees and photographs of her and of my grandfather. I made a special place for them—not knowing what to do with many of them.

And then there is the Lily Dasché hat, a black hat my grandfather picked out for her, with a wide brim, encircled with black ostrich feathers—that I bargained for with my mother—many years before! The hat represents my outrageous grandfather, the stories she shared with me—about him, despite her pain—when I asked!

The diamond came, a gift to her from my grandfather. It became a part of the last Christmas gift from Armin when we went to our favorite jeweler, Gudmund Jos Olsson. He made it, with a very unusual black opal, into a beautiful necklace. I wore it every day and often in that last year Armin would reach up and admire it. I wear it still.

JEAN IN UTAH

THE NECKLACE MADE FROM JEAN'S DIAMOND

37

Jean at her Cabin

Memories

I have so many memories of that trip to Borneo.
    There was a nature preserve
As a part of the resort
    Where they had a feeding station
For the orangutans.
    I asked for help from one of the rangers
And he put his arm around Jean's waist,
    Her arm over his shoulder
And walked her up the jungle trail
    Over the roots,
Impossible for her to do alone,
    To see the orangutans feeding.
She said, "I thought I was going to stay
      At the hotel and you were going
      To see the orangutans.
I replied,
     "I didn't bring you half way around the world
     To sit in the hotel!"

We flew to another place where they had created
    A sanctuary to save the orangutans
From the destruction of their environment
    As civilization gave way to farming.
We walked the beautiful pathway
    And we spent a long time,
Watching and learning
    About these amazing animals
Who would steal bright red purses!

As the orangutans became accommodated
     To the preserve,
They are moved further back into the wild
     Where they eventually live
As close as possible to their natural way,
     Feeding themselves, raising their young,
Exploring their world high in the tree-tops.

It was a memorable adventure
     Learning in all kinds of ways
And about the orangutans.

44

June

It is June.
      I still turn on the lights
But Armin now accepts and understands
      The meaning of my morning ritual.
And only sometimes goes around when I am gone
      To turn them down again,
Responding to his father's lifelong admonishment
      To turn off the lights.
He has softened his compulsion
      By knowing what it means to me.

After a lifetime of being a night person
      Moving into high gear as the sun goes down,
I am becoming a morning person
      At least in the summer time
When the light is beautiful
      And I have so much to do in my garden
Or to capture the morning light with my camera.

There are not enough hours in the day now
      To satisfy my inner excitement and agendas
But it is all different—
      Painting, photography, writing,
         And gardening
            Consume my energy
      As I explore and indulge in life in new ways.

I still write Morning Pages
      And sometimes poetry in the morning.

I have to remember now to write the poems
        To capture my experiences,
Where before, I could not contain
        The deluge of feelings and loss.

I have been reading Sarah's books
        About Simple Abundance
And find many things for which I am deeply grateful
        While gaining new insights
For my authentic and abundant life.

Last year I began photography courses
        With anxiety about myself and the new.
Now we are planning
        For a new photography adventure
In our favorite place of Provence.
        I am dreaming about a new camera
And the process of my work.
        I am seeing in new ways,
Which somehow express that part of me
        That is whole and growing and giving.

My garden was beautiful in the spring
        And is still so in the summer.
I work hard at learning to care for it,
        Paying attention to the plants I use
To learn what each needs.
        It is a delight to find new things blooming
Surprising me with their return,
        Affirming the choices I had made
And the talents of my garden design friend.

I hate to leave my garden.
  I miss a whole phase of its beauty
While I am traveling on my adventures
  To distant lands of Borneo and Provence,
Connecting my friends of past with present
  And creating new memories with my love.
Our family is still in far away places
  Connecting only for moments
And in small ways, but reminding each other
  That we have a special bond of family
In many ways, large and small.
  I miss them and long for more,
Feeling the pain—but it passes
  As I focus on other things
Which make my days joyful and complete.
  I miss my mother
And feel her loss again,
  As we travel to cemeteries to paint
Or record in my photographs
  The ways people remember
Those who have gone before.

We are not there yet to the poignant days of July,
  My Mother's birthday,
Marking the beginning of those fateful events—
  Her 80th birthday, illness and death
Which made such an impact on my life.
  But I feel it all anew
As my closest friend experiences
  The illness and death of her mother
And I can only say—*I've been there too.*

PARENTS OF
GRACE FRANCES
ROBERTA ANN
CORALIE RUTH
JAMES PAUL
JEANINE

JEANINE HARLOW
1945 — 1951
5 YRS. 8 MO. 12 DA.

Work

My life of work is changing.
　　While I enjoyed the teaching,
My return is to a past
　　That no longer exists
As a lively, growing part of me
　　But only a painful reminder
Of something that consumed and used up
　　My inner heart and dreams.
My feelings are changing
　　As I want to leave this past
As completely as my condo which is now gone
　　With only traces that once expressed
An important part of me.

Now my studio holds these special moments
　　Of my life at various stages.
The colors that I love, the work I do,
　　Creating a beautiful place in my home.

I loved the fireplace in the winter
　　And the magic
Of turning on the instant flame
　　And heat to go with it
　　　　To warm my soul and feet
As I sat beside it dreaming, writing, working.
　　Now my favorite place is a table
I have placed beside the French doors
　　That open into the tree.
The breeze soothes me,

The scene providing the visual treats
     Of color and peacefulness
Which define this special place.
          I have explored new worlds of painting,
Creating new visual images
          Arising from my interior life
And consuming my energy
          With the physicality of it all.
It leaves me, as does my gardening,
          Tired and able to sleep at night.

My house is becoming orderly
          As I quiet the raging beasts inside
Disposing of some things I no longer need.
          The dreams still come
But I am not so afraid of them,
          Recognizing them
As the work of my restless mind
          Playing havoc with my sleeping.
But all is a part of this process
          Of my inner life unfolding.

The future is only in shapes
          As I venture to new places.
I have an image of the new camera I want
          But I will have to save my money for it
And create a time to learn to use it
          Slowly and quietly as I explore my worlds.
I have to get another car, a station wagon,
          If I am going to continue with my painting
Of large canvases

53

55

56

And hauling my photography equipment
       As I venture to new places.

I love the freedom
       Of dressing in my gardening clothes
Or showing up in my painting clothes
       Or wearing my funny sun hat and dark glasses
Looking like a creature from outer space,
       Unconcerned with my appearance,
Nor in a role that once defined my life.

These feelings of excitement and fear
       Create a crisis as I bubble over with energy
Pouring out my stored-up process
       As I move into new realms
Of endings and beginnings.
       Grateful for all I have—
Including those with whom I share
       This newly unfolding life and parts of me.

I can breathe more easily now
       Knowing I am past the worst—and safe,
And can face the present and the future,
       Generating new life and energy
Inside of me.

Conflict

I feel so down,
     So hopeless that I will ever get it right
To be able to live with another in peaceful
     Coexistence, nurturing ourselves
And each other in joy and growth.

The most casual situation
     Even in the midst of contentment
Can bring out the sharp biting poke of the past
     Without warning or time to hide
My openness.

I feel as if there will never be a place
     Where I can live in peace
Without the pain of conflict
     Searing through my existence.

It is hard to see the possibility for growth
     In such encounters.
They seem so final, so unchanging,
     So irreversible, the past so powerful,
Beyond change.

Yet in those small encounters
     Lie the possibilities
That we can grow beyond the past
     Into a new kind of living
       We both imagined
        Together.

Questions

I hate questions!
      They are so intrusive
Into my private feeling world
      A place no one has a right to enter
Unless I choose to share the parts of me
      Residing there.
No one seems to realize
      That questions are a safe way
For them to interact
      While making the other vulnerable.

One does not expose one's inner world
      When asking a question
That may penetrate
      The most painful private world of another,
Made worse by knowing
      The other is untouched, elusive,
Even evasive,
      Behind their wall.
It makes me angry
      To feel so exposed this way.

The world I live in
      Seems to think that asking questions
Is as fundamental as eating white bread.
      I see the value and power of questions
To inform about facts,
      But I find them so uncomfortable
In my own private feeling world

And notice that others also seem
    To withhold their own inner world
When they ask questions.

This issue of questions haunts me.
    I try to make it clear
To people close to me
    How painful it is to have them intrude
Into this private feeling world
    Where I experience my own unique way
Of being.

Some find ways I can tolerate more easily
    By asking permission to ask questions
And even limit them to a specified few.
    This "advance permission" helps me
To feel less invaded
    And gives me control of the gates
To my inner world.

But for others it is their way of being in the world
    To ask questions, hiding, yet defending it
As their own way of learning about others,
    Never realizing they intrude
Without risking their own vulnerability.

I feel so defensive, as if I must always be on guard
    Outside the medieval walls of my inner world
Protecting the gates from invasion
    By these unknown, untrusted strangers,
Even those I, on the surface, know well.

Shared Intimacy

So many people seem unaware
      Of the beautiful process of shared intimacy
When the river flows smoothly.
      As two people interact openly,
Each joining the flow,
      They can open the gates of their inner worlds
And share freely as trust and intimacy build.

I wish I knew how to facilitate this flow
      And opening of my self
That we might join each other by sharing freely
      Our mutual inner selves,
Feeling the coming together of our separate selves—
      Connecting.

Congruence between my inner and outer selves
      Seems to be the key
If only I can be myself.
      This open process between us
May follow and become the connecting
      Of our separate inner lives
Into a momentary one
      Which remains between us,
Even as we part.

Older Friends

I have collected older friends over the years
     People who have been a part of my life
In different ways—touching me with their wisdom
     And years in special ways.
I have gained so much from them.

Now all of a sudden, I feel so vulnerable.
     Their years remind me that they will leave me
And I am aware of how vulnerable I have become
     In admitting their importance in my life
As I face this inevitability of loss.

I went to visit Rozella
     And found her
          Preparing to give up her home.
She talked about the reasons—
     Growing too old to live alone,
Her loss of vision and hearing
     And not wanting to cook.
She used a phrase in her decision which I enjoy,
     "I have to get the consent of my mind."

She provides a mirror for me
     To look through between now and then
What do I want my life to be about
     In the twenty-two years that lie between
My age now and hers.

ROZELLA SCHLOTFELDT

Courtesy of Frances Payne Bolton School of
Nursing, Case Western Reserve University

She has been a heroine to me
    And tells me now she wants me
To have something from her home—
    I am touched.
She has heard my wish, a lovely plate of violets.
    I know just where it will go.
And then as I leave
    She mentions the rocking chair and I say
"Let's see if it will go in my car."

And now her rocking chair
    Keeps me company in my studio
And two of her many hoods
    Bestowed through honorary degrees.

I hope someday to work with her work
    And be able to share with new generations
The visions she had from her inquiring mind.
    These friends also bring gifts to me
But they are of a different sort,
    Showing me the struggles of changing health,
Of giving up homes
    Living in new arrangements for the elderly
With all the dramas of collective living
    (Which I have heard about from Jean
All these years).

I see their interests changing too
    Sometimes in exactly the ways they have
Given to me, leaving behind what is no longer real
    In their new place in life.
These friends show such courage in facing losses
    Reminding me their frailty is only physical,
Their courage strong.
    I cherish our times together
And the mementos they share with me
    Taking up a new residence in my home
Providing a connection between us
    In a now new way.

I will lose them one day
 As life follows its relentless, irrevocable,
Inexorable path.
 But I will remember them
In the special ways we have shared
 And in the gifts they leave behind

* * * * * * * * *

Postscript:

I visited Rozella in her lovely new apartment in an old building in the heart of the university district she loved, Case Western Reserve. She had kept two of my photographs and I found them there, hanging on her walls. I had dinner with her in their dining room and saw how respected and cared for she was by others there, as well as by her friends and colleagues of long years.

Later,

The memorial service for her was touching in many ways—respectful of all her gifts she had shared with the school and the nursing world in which she led so long before. I still see her as the most imminent and visionary scholar in nursing in my lifetime. Students and colleagues who spoke made it clear their respect and admiration for her also.

Her phrase, "the consent of my mind," stays with me.

ROZELLA'S ROCKING CHAIR WITH
HOODS FROM HONORARY DEGREES

Gifts

I have a tremendous ring of support around me.
> People who have come into my life

At different times in various ways,
> Are here for me now.

Each in his or her own way, reminds me
> That I am loved

And that my world can be a caring one.

No one can do this work for me.
> Sometimes they cannot even enter

The battlefields I must face.
> But it makes a tremendous difference

Knowing they are here and I can reconnect
> With them

Even when I am too alone to care.

At first, they sent gifts of new ideas
> Or made their presence felt by being there.

We were able to do things with friends
> Even when the fun was muted

By the sadness I felt.
> (In compassion, they didn't even comment).

But their gifts brought new images
> Like hot air balloons lifting off the ground,

Each with gifts of love and possibility.

FIRST MEETING GRACE AND ARMIN
Qaxtepec, Mexico, June 1982
Photos: Jean Clark

70

Armin

It was in a special place that first we met.
      Far from the madding crowd they say,
The unusual can happen.

The single strand in each our lives,
      A man named Carl,
Woven into the core of its fabric
      Brought two strangers from different worlds
Together in an exotic place
      As if it were all intended.

It seemed so natural at first
      To see someone interesting, sitting near,
I reached out and introduced myself
      Never imagining I was changing my life
          Forever.

I noticed he stayed close by
      Without realizing it was by design.
It was a long time before he admitted
      He was like a moth, attracted to the light,
Unable to let it go.
      And so, he told stories to make it seem
All unintended.

We walked the paths of beautiful flowers,
      We talked about our lives,
The special interest that had brought us
      To a gathering far away.

He told me about his special house
    Almost before about himself
Except that it was about himself.

The time was long enough
    To bring two worlds together
Far from those of our daily lives
    And plans were made to meet again.

He called the day I was to have arrived home,
    Free of the relationship
He had been unhappy in.
    He asked me to meet him in Toronto
And when I arrived
    He had made a sign
The Second International Meeting
    Of the Grace-Armin Approach!

The die was cast!

He wrote poetry to me in October
    And gave it to me when I came to visit him.

I found a letter he had saved from the same time—
    Here is how we can do it!
He the poetic one, I the doing, more practical one!

Tenderness

What is this deep and overwhelming tenderness?
    I thought it our creation.
Or your gift to me—starved as I was.
    But that would make us precious—
Or me unworthy.

I sense our tenderness is a vast echoing cathedral,
    A place of reverence—opening.
A place we too stubborn, determined explorers
    Have sought forever.
Driven by unconscious visions
    And encouraged by but partial successes,
A place we were unable to enter alone.

Now with you, I am awestruck
    As we walk together in this new world.
Everything is here, even more memories.

Our tenderness is a hallowed place.

    It is a way of being.

A way of being that transforms my life.

    Armin Klein
    1982

I asked him to share the poem
     In the group of family and friends
Who came to bless our marriage,
     Bringing together so much of our old lives,
Connecting with the new.
     Our friends, Don and Vivian Weilerstein
Played a beautiful concert for us—
     The music Armin so loved
         Throughout his life.

It was a beautiful summer day
     As we gathered in our backyard.
Our friends, Lois and Bill , married just a year,
     Came to be with us.
Jane played her harp.
     Many spoke of the places shared in our lives.
Murray recited the old Shakespeare Sonnet,

"Let me not to the marriage of true minds admit
impediments." #116

Our friends, Bill, and Sr. Mary Kay came to
"officiate" and gave their blessings.

For a day the struggles dropped away,
     Leaving the love alone
To bind us in our marriage
     Of equals and battle-scarred veterans.

We invited our children to join us
     But knew it was too late for them

To be at the center of a family.
    The barriers of distance,
Of different cultures,
    Of children born and raised
In different families
    Remain.
Brought together only by our love,
    The others must find their places,
Each, as best they can.

The path was sometimes difficult
    To cross the boundaries of separate lives
And work and families and cultures
    Far different from our own.
We are different.

What kept the flame alive
    Was knowing we had met a soulmate.

We shared the inner values, hopes and visions,
    Of relationships, feelings, communication,
Of connection, respecting each other,
    While love grew.

We could always talk!
    Sitting in the library,
Which was the place of Armin's work,
    I always took his big chair
When we asked to talk!

Somehow being heard
    Changed the perspective
That stood in our way
    Freeing the flow between us
Once again,

The struggles were painful,
    The challenges many.
The doubts reappear
    With each new threshold to be crossed.
But still the love endures.
    And I am glad to have his company
On my life's journey.

We have celebrated the marriages of children
    Choosing their own partners.
The births of grandchildren
    Open new doors for shared love
While distance continues to make it harder
    To be together.

The loss of loved ones has brought grief
    Along with dreams, deep in hearts.
The knowledge that his parents will never know
    The joys of our marriage is sad,
As is the reality that we will not have children
    To celebrate our union.

Despite and through it all,
    We grow in love.

Within ourselves we heal old wounds,
      Open new doors,
Explore new lands,
      Face aging and death
Together, still in love.

Dedicated to Carl R. Rogers
who was the single strand.

Photo: Carol Wolter-Gustafson

OUR WEDDING CELEBRATION
AUGUST 20, 1983

SHAKATI SINGH, UPKAR

TIM, MOLLY, JANEY, MEG

JOHN, KELLY, BOBBY

LISA, KATIE, JACOB, CHRIS

KEITH, CAITRIN, CINDY, MAIREAD

Thomas

The Kitchen

I can never forget "the kitchen" Armin wanted to
     Renovate before our wedding.
Of course, the contractor promised
     It would be finished two weeks ahead—
And, of course, it was not!

I look back on our adventure to say,
     We didn't know each other well enough
To undertake something so huge!
     We hadn't even talked about our finances.
But we did.

And out of all that chaos
     The dark, cobbled up area
Became a glorious kitchen—
     With cherry wood beams and posts
And cabinets—
     Huge French doors opening to the back
     That lit up the space
And invited us onto our back porch
     For eating—all the summers that we had—
Even when Armin was in a wheelchair.

The rocks from the back wall
     Became the first border for my garden
     Which has grown over the years
     With beautiful flowering trees
     Tree peonies of gorgeous colors,
     Peonies—and hydrangeas!

We made decisions that lasted
     For the kitchen
        For us
For our world of work
     Inviting others into our space
        Of love and warmth and healing.

The kitchen became the gathering place
     Along with the dining room table
For family and friends for all the years we had.

After Armin died, in desperate need for light,
    I made one change—
And put a white wall covering with silver trees
    That stand out in brightness,
        Reflecting the light.

Escape

Our wedding was on Saturday—
    We spent the night alone—
        Exhausted and in ecstasy.

Meg left for graduate school on Sunday
Along with our friends from far away places.

The workmen returned on Monday!

We said, "We have to get out of here.!"

    Our friends,
Joanne and Bruce came to the rescue.
    She had a relative with a cottage
On the Jersey shore—
    A quiet place on the bay,
Only a block from the beach.

We arrived—
    To a bottle of champagne
    In the refrigerator.

For a week we relaxed—
    Just the two of us.
Heaven!
    My first photographs
Of Armin, my beloved husband.

Paris at night

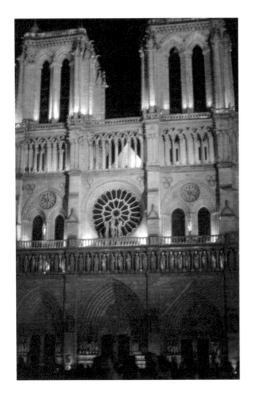 

Provence

This is an incredible time in Provence
    When I am learning to see with new eyes
And passion for beauty and light.
    I awaken in the night and try to capture
The dark blue night sky and the two stars visible
    From our window which move so persistently
Across the skyscape and then are gone.
    I often stay awake
To catch the morning light as well
    Playing on the walls and bedclothes
Creating fascinating moments of illusion
    When time stands still and there are only
Light and shadows making feast for my eyes
    And for my imagination.

In the midst of it all I am learning as well
    To understand how to manipulate my camera
To discover what it will do when I adjust
    Its various buttons or try the different lens,
Making variations of what I see possible.
    I could get used to this life
Where ideas and images fill my head.
    I find myself ordering my days
Around the incredible morning and evening
    Light of Provence,
Sharing the companionship of my love
    And the wonderful food and wines
Of Provence.

I sleep soundly, if only for a while
    So as not to waste this wonderful time.

I made myself sick with the stress of leaving
    (And had to have a colonoscopy
Before my physicians would let me go).
    I lost a day in Paris
Along with my energy to explore.
    But I was determined to leave,
Somehow knowing this long-awaited time
    Was a key to my love of photography
And the continuing evolving of my life.

I remember the first time I saw the paintings
    Of Van Gogh in Washington, D.C.
And the incredible change
    From the darkness of the poor
In his Dutch homeland
    To the light of his paintings of Provence.
In this land he traveled
    Creating such intense and beautiful visions
Of the world of his passions.
    Seeing his paintings began to awaken
My visual world
    Unknown to my awareness.

Over the years I have traveled many places
    And managed to see Van Gogh's paintings
        In Paris, at home,
    And in the museum created for his work
        In Amsterdam—Twice!

99

Knowing the sadness of his short life,
      I somehow feel his world of feelings
Through his wonderful paintings.

And all the while I carried a camera,
      Recording snapshots of family events
Until I saw Rich's photographs
      And said, *I want to do that.*
Dean gave me my first real camera
      And the world exploded as I traveled.
Learning to see and record the places and what I saw
      I wondered why I had wasted so many years
Without a good camera.

Now we are here in Saint-Rémy
      Visiting the Clinique where Van Gogh spent
The last year of his life.
      We see his room and I take a photo,
Wanting to remember the simplicity of this place.

We walk the paths they have created
      Marking the paintings he did in each place.
I feel my own world turning and emerging
      In new forms.
It is a prelude to what is becoming—
      A life of art and photography
And writing of my experience,
      A feeling world of pain and beauty
Amidst the tragedy of other lives.
      The tragedy of Van Gogh's short intense life
Of always feeling a failure,

Supported only by his brother
        Was in the end not enough
To hold back the ravages of his mind.
        He ended his life, himself,
Never really knowing that his art
        Would touch millions of people,
                Including me.

The world of tragedy is made real
        By Kathy's portraits of the children of Africa
Orphaned by the millions of people with Aids.
        The consequences for children,
None of it their doing, nevertheless
        Reduces their life's options
To almost nothing.

The story of the children has an enormous impact
        On Armin.
Only three years the children live,
        When left as orphans
On the streets to fend for themselves
        Through all manner of ungodly activities.
"Three Years of Dying" was Armin's poem,

Reliving his own childhood tragedy
        Of a family blown apart,
Taking his father away.
        Ill with pneumonia at eight,
His physician told his father
        "Junie* is dying."
            *Armin's childhood family name, after his father.

And finally his father came home.
    Junie thought his father was dead,
Leaving him with a very distraught
    And angry mother.

Though he has struggled with his relationship
    With his mother all his life,
His poem is the first time he put all of it together—
    What had happened to him.

My own small tragedy, in the death of my sister,
    Though just as real,
Shrinks in proportion to both the stories
    Of the children in Africa
And that of young Junie.

It begins to feel like the closing of a door.
    However violently it happened,
I have used the opportunity to open many new ones
    That now are beginning to take form
And give direction for my life with new meaning.

Our Time in Provence

Each day at the workshop
    We went to another village
        To take photographs.
Several places are in the book
    The Most Beautiful Villages in Provence.
Craig Stevens, the leader of the workshop,
    Has done this for many years
        And knows the best places to go.

By late afternoon we are finished—
    Turning in our film slides to be developed—
Ready for the next day.
    We spend time together
    Looking at our work from the day before.
Craig gives us feedback—
    Things to pay attention to
In order to make our work better.
    By four the light is better—
A perfect time for more photographs.

The people at the hotel are generous
    With suggestions for great places to eat—
This land of France where food and wine
    Are so appreciated.

We go alone to be together
    And enjoy each new restaurant—

Wonderful food
    And wine which Armin especially enjoys.
He becomes the wine consultant for our group!
    It is a marvelous time
Armin and I together
    And a time of great exploration and learning.

One of my favorite photographs came from here
    Abbey de Senaque, a very old monastery
With the beautiful field of lavender,
    The inspiration for a new addition
To my garden.

Two Lines Up Eccentric

I saw a sculpture on my walk
    Waving its arms in the air
Moving hither and there in random ways.
    It caught my eye as I stopped to watch
The sun catching it in many of its planes
    Glowing like sparkling water on its face.
Two lines made of metal
    Two Lines Up Eccentric—it was named
The arms move up twelve feet then sideways
    Never stopping, never touching.
This looks just like I feel, I cried.
    I wonder if George Rickey* felt like me.

My life feels as random as these arms look
    Moving in different directions
Never coming together or stopping.
    But as I watched, another thought emerged.

These arms move in perfect balance,
    One offsetting the other.
They keep the movement flowing
    Without ever knowing where it is going.

I like that version of where I want to be
    In perfect balance inside of me
While free to explore and keep on going
    To wherever my dreams
Take this growing part of me
                  *the sculptor

George Rickey
American

TWO LINES UP
EXCENTRIC —
TWELVE FEET
1991
Stainless Steel

Gift of Richard F. Brush, 94.44

Bats in My Belfry, Would You Believe

I am terrified of bats in my house.
    Their swooshing and flying
Seem like frantic evidence of their experience
    Of being caught in a place
Where they do not belong—
    And from which there is no escape.
It feels like some aspects of my life—
    And brings out all my feelings
Of helplessness and fear.
    Over the years we have such visitors.
We can never figure out how they enter
    And since their visits are rare,
We stop worrying about it when they are gone.

Once we talked with the friendly exterminators
    But they could offer no help and so
Armin learned a new use for his tennis racket
    Which allows him to kill them in flight.

A month ago I began to suspect there was a bat
    Living in the rafters of my studio.
I had left the door open one night
    Without the screen being shut
And when I went upstairs
    I suddenly felt the familiar swooshing sound
And saw the bat flying around.
    When I saw the telltale droppings,
I began to suspect the bat had taken up residence!
    I was not pleased.

Then one night I turned on the light
    In my darkened bedroom and there
Was my friendly bat, swooshing and flying.
    I quickly shut the door
    And waited for my favorite bat killer
    To come home—
    Thinking—at least we've got the bat.

Wrong! I cleaned up everything in my studio
    And within an hour there were new signs
Of that bat in the rafters—again.
    I finally asked my husband
To consult, once again,
    Our friends the exterminators
And he agreed to do that the next day.

That night I stayed behind in the kitchen
    While he went up to bed
And suddenly there was the bat in my kitchen
    And the whole scenario
Was played out once again.

As I went to bed I decided to check
    And see if my studio doors were still closed
Trying to determine if this now dead bat
    Had any possibility of being the bat
Which had been living in my studio.

When the doors were shut, I opened them slowly
    Onto the swooshing flying bat—

And I once again called for my husband
     Who arrived with his tennis racket.
We turned on the lights
     To find two bats swooshing and flying
Through the air!
     Now I know that bats are protected species
Who do good, but I also know they carry rabies
     And want to know who is going to protect ME
From these crafty flying creatures.

So my husband did his magic
     Making him my all time hero
Of killing three bats in one night.
     And I became the grateful wife
Rescued by his skill and bravery.

The moral of this tale of woe of bats
     Who dared to enter my sacred studio—
And found their end
     Lies only in my head.

I ponder the illogical, unplanned,
     Unreasonable, uncontrollable,
Unexplainable in my life,
     Brought on by these bats in my studio—
Who really had no other vice
     Except to be in the wrong place
With someone terrified of bats in my house.

My Calendar Clock

For over thirty years and change
　　　My life ran on a special kind of clock
A beginning in August and ending in May.
　　　Although there were small changes
Through the years
　　　The importance was the sameness,
Reinforcing the importance of my life's work
　　　In learning.
For some of those years I was a student
　　　But for most of them I was the teacher,
Involved in young lives growing toward new dreams.
　　　My dream was to be a part of the process.

I marked the seasons by small things,
　　　The flowers which bloomed in August
Saying the time is near—
　　　Learning the rhythm of students' progress
So that I no longer felt the panic in their learning,
　　　That they would never "get it"—
The feverish pace of the "red zone"
　　　A student once called it—
Before the time of celebration.

At the end was the recognition of accomplishments
　　　And appreciation for gifts given,
Support provided.
　　　Celebration of another new generation
　　　　　Launched and on its way,
Marked the permanence for those of us who stayed.
I have never been afraid to dream
　　　To pit my talents and energy

Toward something better than what I saw.
    I heard my own drummer
And attempted to follow it.
    Sometimes people joined me
With their dreams and for brief moments
    We felt the synchrony
Of our shared energy.

But always there were those
    Who had different agendas.
It wasn't enough to pursue their own dreams.
    Many said,
"Your dreams are not as important as ours;
    You must give more to make ours better
Because ours is the star."

I no longer want to be a part of that world,
    The dream lost in the crashing wave.
I see the continuation by others
    Who still believe.
But my dreams have changed
    And as each day unfolds
I see them opening before me.
    My calendar is now marked in new ways
With the fullness of my life and my dreams
    Which no one can take away
Until I have lived it to its end.

MY DAD AND THE CLOCK HE
MADE FOR EACH OF US

Burning Out or Winding Down

We have a fan, only one year old.
    Without warning, it stopped working.
When I turn it on, I can hear the noise of the motor
    But the blades turn almost imperceptibly.
If I wait long enough, with the switch on High
    It seems to gather energy and begin to turn
A bit more. And finally it reaches its full speed,
    And runs normally until it is shut off.
The next time I turn it on,
    The process begins all over again.
I can't help but think the fan is dying,
    Burning out of its own effort to start the cycle
All over again.

I feel like the fan,
    Burning out from the effort to live my life
Which has so little natural energy being generated
    By its own internal combustion.
I am exhausted.
    There have been too many obligations,
Too few joys.
    Even my efforts at exercise
Which supposedly generate energy
    Leave me unable to go through the motions
Once again the next day.

There have been too many people
    With whom I feel so little connection.

The weather has been so hot
        I could barely keep my garden watered
Much less enjoy the gardening itself.

Everything seems like too much effort
        To even get out of bed
Yet I continue going through the motions.

I feel like the clock winding down, as well.
        The weights are touching the bottom
And I cannot lift them to restart the process
        For an endless number of times.

I awakened from a dream, feeling this way.
        I know it reflects how I felt
When I went to bed.
        I was being terminated from my job
Along with all my colleagues
        In all the ignominy of absolute invisibility.
I left, carrying out a laundry basket of nothing
        But the last junk left.
I was wearing an old robe, not really dressed
        For others to see,
But there I was, leaving,
        Having to walk by others in that state.
It reminds me of dreadful images of the Holocaust.
        They knew with dread what was coming.
I just feel embarrassed and wish I were invisible.

Others spoke of their reorganizing efforts,
　　That this was the result of only a few
Believing they could find new masters
　　Or even the same one,
Willing to continue the charade.

I feel a strange sense of freedom as I write,
　　My perspective shifting,
The fear and embarrassment easing.
　　Sustained by many charades,
I am letting this clock wind down to nothing.

When there is only me and the world I have
　　Outside my work.
It is primarily a world of people
　　Sustained by the relationships
I have with them.
　　I even think I might like this self
And my ways of being in this world
　　I have created.
But first there must be time
　　To just be.

Remaking a Life

Armin took the fan apart yesterday.
    I came upstairs and saw all the parts
Lying on the floor.
    The oil can stood among them.
Later he said the fan was fixed.
    When I went to bed I pressed the On button
And the fan immediately began to turn
    And moved into its cycle
At only the speed of 2—generating more air
    Than it had done before on High.

I am trying to do the same for my self,
    Taking apart the events and feelings of my life
Reinspecting each once again
    Trying to find the peace and freedom
That will allow me to function freely
    In this new world I occupy.

Each day is a test of resilience and empowerment.

We bought new hanging baskets for the porch.
    They were lined with a kind of fiber mat
Inside the metal frame.
    They looked much prettier
Than the white plastic pots
    We had used before.
But I had to learn the new requirements
    For watering, a little water,
Poured all around the plants, not the jug

124

Dumped in that would fill the pot,
      Spreading the water through the roots.
But before I figured it out
      In the hottest days of summer
The potting soil turned to concrete
      And many of the plants died.
I bought new plants
      And tried to water them each day until
I summoned the time and energy
      To tackle a new task.

Yesterday I took the baskets down,
      Waiting until the cool of evening
So the plants would not be as shocked
      By their moving and repotting
And began the process of remaking them.
      It wasn't so hard to understand
When I got it apart and could see the construction
      Of the baskets, why they required a different
Kind of watering.
      When I replanted them,
Using the plants still alive and the new ones,
      They looked lovely.
And now I understand the requirements
      To keep them healthy and alive.
But it took me hours of getting up my courage
      To tackle the task and then
The hour or so to do it.

Earlier I went to turn on the furnace
        To heat the pool
So I could swim later in the day.
        Usually Armin does this task
And the furnace is new
        So I had not done it this year.
I knew Armin had trouble and had to call Mark
        To come again so I thought I needed to learn
How it works.

I turned it on and it came on and then shut down.
        I turned it off, smelling the gas.
I tried again and then heard the small explosion
        As it lit, the whoosh of noise and then
It shut down again. Finally I figured out
        The meaning of the colors.
The blue range is to start the burner,
        Then it can be
Turned to yellow, orange and red!
        So the heating actually worked
To warm the water of the pool.

Later I swam and enjoyed the water,
        Warmed to take the chill away—
But I also accomplished one more important step
        Of understanding how something works
So that I can be in charge of my world.
        Two tiny steps in an entire day—
And though I allow myself to notice
        I feel overwhelmed by the six others
In front of me in remaking my world

Oh yes, when the gas bill came, I learned
        The cost of heating the pool
And that was the last time I used the heater.
        Now when I swim,
I jump into the cold water and scream!

Did I say that I am challenged technologically?
        I had never even done my own email,
Always having a secretary to act as barrier
        To control my work.

But I have learned some things
        And learned to ask for help.
As recently as yesterday I went
        To the computer store for the second time,
The first had been to get a mouse that worked.
        And then to get the man to fix the connection
                To the WiFi in the house in Provence
Where I am typing this manuscript.
        At first, I got the WiFi to connect—
Le Charmarey—so easily,
        The first time I have ever done that,
And then just as magically, it stopped.

And, of course, there is Robyn in Toronto,
        Who by phone and email and Dropbox
Kept bailing me out of trouble
        Until everything began to work.
What would I do without her?
        I dream of going to Toronto
Sitting on her doorstep until I finish my work!

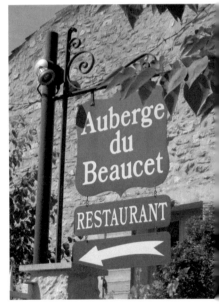

Ambition

"Invite ambition
    To sit down with your authentic Self,"
Wrote Sara on September 19th
    In her daily pages of <u>Simple Abundance</u>.
After giving permission to be ambitious,
    Seeing the possibilities if women
Cherished their ambitions,
    And brought them into the Light
Where they belong,
    She wrote,
"Tell her what you'd like to achieve.
    Listen to her suggestions."*

The door of my mind flew open
    My thoughts cascading through so quickly
My pen could hardly keep up with them.

Dear Ambition,
    I want to publish my books of poetry,
I want them to reach people
    Who are experiencing loss as I have.
I want my poetry to touch them,
    Encourage them that they can survive and
Grow through loss.

I want to speak to people from my books
    Share my poetry with them
Through workshops and work with clients
    Who are experiencing death and loss.

131

I want to write about Empowerment
      And share the power of connection
With other seekers of life's mysteries.

I want to do portraits of people and their lives
      In images and words
Of how they have empowered themselves
      And grown
Through challenges, pain and loss.

I want to see with my camera
      The lights of beauty
And travel to interesting places
      To see the world in all its complexities.
I want to paint,
      To create images of my interior world
Acting as mirrors through which
      Others may see theirs.

I want to have a loving, exciting relationship
      With Armin
And share the life and years we have together
      With our children and grandchildren
And close friends, surrounding ourselves in love
      And community, giving and receiving.

I want to make money in these endeavors,
      Sell my books of poetry,
Hang my photographs and paintings in galleries
      For people to take images home with them
When they speak of their own feelings—

I even want them hung in museums
   Images of interior life
And passions in my own world view.

I want to live comfortably
   And keep my home beautiful.
I want to have money for luxuries
   To make the journey fun.
And enough to share with others
   In ways that have meaning to me.

I have a lot of ambition!
   Why would I not.
It has fueled my dreams all my life
   Brought success from hard work and vision.
I reject the notion of retirement
   Of being defined by my age.
The most exciting part of my life
   Is now and what lies ahead.

Onward! I raise my glass to Ambition
   And roll up my sleeves to get to work.
Action!
   To hell with age.
I am free to pursue my ambitions
   To live my life as fully as I have always done
And more!
   The gifts of age.

*Sarah Ban Breathnach, <u>Simple Abundance</u>, 2000

Opening

I have begun to hope about my future
    To see my poetry printed
My art hung for others to see
    My photographs deepening in vivid colors
And glorious light.

I am terrified by my opening to possibilities
    Of new hopes and dreams.
I feel so vulnerable
    When I think of releasing my jewels
To the universe of others,
    Hoping to find souls like mine
With whom I and we can connect.

I have lived these last years
    Grieving my losses and exploring new paths
In the cloister of my own private world,
    Sharing only parts of it with trusted friends
And all of it with Armin.
    In my own way and time
I have allowed my mind and heart to go back in time
    Over all the losses,
Remembering.
    Crying.
        Writing.
            Healing.
Now I have begun to move through new doors
    Allowing my paintings and poetry

To be seen and read by a few others
  Not quite so close and safe.

The terror comes through
  Without conscious thought
Filling my body with weight and fatigue
  With no clues to help me identify its source.
I have shut down my hope and optimism
  In the terror of being hurt again
Even by people I do not know
  Who will reject my work
Even without reading
  Or seeing the pathway I have walked.

So I am exploring what is happening
  Guided by my Morning Pages writing,
And Julia's pithy comments
  Which bring encouragement and reality
That I can survive these rejections
  And keep moving on to my future
Moment to moment.

Breakthrough

In my discussion with our attorney
    Planning our new center,
A new world opening,
    He asked about the conditions
Of my old world that might constrain the new.
    The discussion led my thinking to Tom,
My attorney who had helped me in my struggle
    With the university.
I asked Tom to find out the state
    Of the lawsuits still remaining.

When we returned home from the weekend
    With our friends in Philadelphia,
I opened the letter from Tom and read,
    "The bottom line of this is that your part
In the lawsuits is now finished."
    My excitement burst through
Three years, four and a half months
    In exhilaration.

Although I did not think of it often this last year,
    It was always there in the back of my mind.
Occasionally it would burst forward
    And I would play over and over,
What I might say if I were called to testify.
    Now it is finished—for me.
Tom also wrote that he would be happy to help me
    With a severance request to the university
If I now desire it.

My euphoria lasted two days,
        Shared with those who love me
And have been with me through all of this.
        Then the fatigue set in—
Visible even to my students—
        Reflecting the weight of the long burden.

The feeling of freedom dances
        Just beyond my awareness,
Held in check by my fear
        And wish to be very clear about the decisions
I now must make—
        To act or not.

To ask for what I want I must decide what I need
        To support my work.
And balance the fear of my vulnerability,
        Exposed by my decisions—
And the act of negotiating with the university.

All of the work I have done
        These forty and a half months
From the very first moment of this debacle's
        Unfolding
Provides the background, foreground
        And solid ground
As I take charge of my life in moving forward.

Remaking a Life

The forced loss of my administrative position
    And Armin's life-threatening illness
Have conspired like a powerful explosive
    To blow open my entire life.
These events demand not just a review,
    But the remaking of my life.

Every rock in the foundation of my life
    Has shifted in these seismic eruptions
And some have disappeared completely,
    Throwing me off-balance into limbo
Demanding that I reexamine everything
    In my daily life and future.

The work is exhausting
    And I encounter many hurdles
That set off my feelings
    Of overwhelming helplessness
And frustration.

But as I proceed, one step at a time,
    I move forward,
Mostly knowing only as I look back to where I was
    That I am no longer there.

Now I am making a huge decision
    That will effect everything in my future.
I have proposed to the university
    A plan that will give me two years to write

Followed by my retirement.
    I am frightened
By the enormity of this decision.
    Now there would be an opportunity
    And no excuses for not dong the writing.

Will I meet this challenge
    I have given myself?
Will I meet the fear and move through it?
    I know I have something important to say
But will I take the risk of exposing my ideas
    To others? I hope so.
I am also excited
    That I could focus my energy on this agenda
And expand beyond it
    With my other creative work.

I have worked long to fund my life
    And my retirement.
Now we have created the structure
    Of a business, a dream we had long ago
That would give a focus to continuing our work
    Together into a new phase
With ongoing possibilities for income.
    I have observed that many others
Combine their work around ideas and writing,
    Lectures and workshops in various forms
And individual and group therapy clients
    Which Armin has always had.
Now I am embarking on a similar path.

The loss of funds in my retirement
    Has made the sense of risk greater,
But I am trying to live with equanimity
    As I move into this last phase
Of working for the university
    And begin to work for myself.

It is hard to anticipate the future
    When it is so uncertain.
One part of me longs to stay
    In this known world
Despite all its discomforts
    And non-recognition of me.
But the growing part of me
    Pushes onward, into this unknown,
Claiming my life for myself
    And freedom from others
In the institution.

I have lived by the school calendar for sixty years!
    Since I began kindergarten at age five,
Every August–September
    Has been the start of the year
And every May–June the ending.
    I don't know if my body rhythms can function
Any other way.
    But I want the freedom to try.
I bring many resources and life experiences
    To this new venture—
Skills I have learned in my work for others
    Now I claim to benefit myself and us.

My vision has always been for nursing—
      For schools of nursing—
Now it is for me, for us.

I can only hope that my life experiences
      Of gains and losses through concerted effort
Will carry me to this new place of freedom
      And use of my life's gifts for myself
And for others.
      I am alone—but not alone in this new space.
I am learning to surround myself with friends
      Who care for me.
I stand on the shoulders of my parents
      Who gave so much to me
          And teachers and colleagues
            Who believed in me.
Now I must believe in myself.

My awareness of life's fragility
      Is heightened by Armin's illness.
I realize our time together may be short,
      An awareness
That has helped me to confront
      The sources of separation and pain
That have held us apart.
      As those dissolve,
I find myself relaxing
      Into the possibilities for our future.

We have begun to feel the freedom we would have
      Imagining vacations in quiet times

When others do not travel
　　And being more at home in summer
Which is a beautiful time of year in Rochester.
　　Winter time in the Caribbean,
 Armin imagines would be a wonderful time
　　And place for workshops
In a beautiful place of relaxation
　　For others and for ourselves.

This freedom is a new thing for me.
　　I have worked as a nurse, teacher and
Administrator for forty five years!

I have the company of Armin
　　As we chart this new phase of our lives
　　　Together.

The I and He remain separate
　　But the We is growing as the barriers fade.
A new life is dawning and I imagine
　　The explorations will be wonderful.

I long to hold on to our home
　　That I have made mine
And my beautiful garden.
　　I hope to use my studio for my work
And sitting room for my work with clients.
　　Some days I feel as if I have prepared well.
Other days I fear it could all disappear—
　　Like so many other losses in my life.

Divorce

It is like a divorce, this process I am entering,
        Negotiating with the university
Terms leading to our separation.
        In the world of charades, it is called
Retirement.
        But I think divorce is closer to the reality.

We have mostly moved beyond the hatred
        To indifference.
Only occasionally does the old hatred return,
        Rearing on hind legs like a stallion.
We are even pretending to be polite and civil
        When under the surface we have no use
For each other and can only negotiate the terms
        Of separation.

The dreams and fantasies have long died for me
        Lost in a thousand small betrayals
And a huge one that brought the end.
        The students I loved are caught up too
In a new kind of disillusionment
        And the effort is too great
To try to help them hold on to their dreams
        In an environment no longer part
Of my own dreams.
        It is time for the end.

I do not know what will come
  When I have cut myself free
From this structure called the university
  Where I have lived
Almost all of my working life.
   I understand most clearly
Armin's dislike for institutions,
  Having experienced his own disillusionment.
And I am more angry
  With what they have done to him
Than for myself.
  I was, at least, on the payroll.

I still love the university of my dreams
  Where learning is the focus and source
Of new ideas and passions.
  It has meant so much to my growing life
And learning about myself.
  But it was my energy and dreams
That fueled that process
  And mingled with the energy and dreams
Of others whom I met along the way
  That made my life grow.

Now I must take my own battered self away
  And let my soul find new dreams
And new energy to create
  A new life for me.

Dream

In my dream I was on an escalator
     A long, long one,
          Descending into the ground
Like the Metro station in Washington, D. C.
     Lisa was five and she came from behind me
Falling.

I tried to catch her, but couldn't get hold of her
     And she lay on the concrete at the bottom
When I reached her,
     Still, but breathing.

I was frightened, terrified,
     As I have been for so long in my life.
The images and feelings cross many boundaries—
     Jeanine's fall,
Even though I was not there,
     Her death, my terror,
Aloneness.

But as I stay with my dream,
     I hear Jim saying yesterday,
"It was too painful,"
     When I said I hadn't been able
To stay open to my art when Armin got sick.
     I had said it made me too vulnerable
To be in my art, feeling everything inside of me
     Not monitoring what came out—
Sometimes not even knowing what it was—

Until it was on my canvas,
    Visible to me.
But Jim is more accurate
    And now I feel the fear inside of me.

For a few moments I open to the depths of it.
    But it is far too intense to stay with it.
I feel the reserve I have known so long
    Closing over the fear,
Creating the mask of control and poise
    I carry so well.

I share bits of it with Armin
    And he asks if I am afraid of him.
"Yes," I nod.
    But this feeling is very old
Going back in some way to my mother
    And then the painful intrusions of relatives
Who judge and embrace and fawn—
    Without recourse—
When I am uncomfortable with it all.

It is as if I have always felt unsafe at times.
    And unable to protect myself
From these unwanted intrusions
    Into my inner world,
Leaving me feeling helpless, powerless
    In this most fundamental space
        Inside of me.

It is not always this way,
       But maybe far more than I realize
I remember the clashing household
       Of family dynamics.
Maybe this is the reason for my reserve
       So strong, so reserved,
So seldom able to let anything out spontaneously—
       Except perhaps in my painting.

I have looked at baby pictures of myself,
       Wondering. Even at age one I had this sense
Of presence inside myself, hiding perhaps,
       The chaos I felt within,
Or simply retreating to a quiet place of safety,
       Exerting my own calm
In an otherwise chaotic world
       That produced so much helplessness.

A family story dates another incident
       Of my awareness. I announced that
"Daddy needs his peace and tiet," at an age
       Before I could speak clearly.
I wonder why I had that awareness.
       Knowing my dad, I am sure it was his need
And that he said it—
       But maybe it was my own peace and tiet
         That I needed.

Today I still am seeking peace and quiet
       Within myself
And in the relationships that surround me.

My search is also reflected in my struggle
      To free myself from the chains
Of institutions and jobs, which, no matter
      How careful my initial agreement,
Seem to evolve into having their teeth
      Into my bodymind and holding on,
Controlling my choices and freedom,
      Just because I am on their payroll.
I finally understand why Armin, having had his own
      Misadventures in institutions
Has so little regard for them.

I am confronting my fears
      In order to leave this old world—
Preparing for my transition to a new way of being
      In my life.

Acknowledgement

My acknowledgement to Armin
        That I was afraid of him
Brought forth his own reflection
        And a beautiful poem.

He said that I was eloquent in my response.
        But this is what I wrote.

Armin and I sat in the library of our home
        Talking quietly
As we have done many times before.
        But something was different.
I told him how frightened I am of being open
        To his chaotic, defensive world.
Even though he tells me often
        How much he loves me
I can not find a place of safety.
        I am so "on the edge," I said,
In trying to make a new life for myself.
        Every sharp pain from our interactions,
Robs me of a piece of hopefulness
        That I can do what lies ahead of me,
Bringing back the feeling,
        "I don't know if I want to live."

I felt as if I had finally said it all
        Baring my inner world
With the struggle I am in
        And have carried so long.

"I am very sad, " I said,
    And fell asleep in the chair.

When I awoke Armin returned
    "I want you to have priority
For what you need,
    And I want you to tell me what it is."

As we prepared supper, Armin said,
    "I am sad."
"I too," I said.

It was a very intimate time
    As we felt the pain
We have experienced in our relationship.
    The sadness seemed to be for each of us.

We began with so much hope and optimism
    And have experienced such joy together.
But always the pain returned
    Taking away in its presence
        Some piece of hope.

But in this sadness there is a knowing
    And intimacy with our own truths
About the pain of the struggle
    To reach this place of openness.
And now that we are here
    The sadness sits like a sentinel
Reminding us of the pain and loss and cost.

150

Fear Unbounded

I am afraid of life.
 I am afraid to be happy—
To let go of everything into the flow.
 Is it holding on to the fear
Or knowing the risk, risk anyway.

There are no guarantees
 That life will be good—or bad.
It is more likely to be a mixture
 Changing from moment to moment
Through every day.

Somehow the challenge is to trust oneself
 And those whose love is secure
To be there when you fall
 And rejoice when you succeed.

I brought Bill the picture of himself,
 Caught in a moment of ease.
He was sitting on his deck, alone
 To smoke his cigar,
Bundled up in winter clothes
 Under the umbrella covered with snow.

Christmas

It is Christmas once again and I am lost.
  I wandered through my favorite stores
(Minus the one that closed this year),
  Looking for the spirit to hit me

But it didn't.
  My children are coming
Bringing their children.
  But something is missing
The excitement gone or hiding.

I miss my parents, the family I grew up in
  And with whom my Christmas memories
Were born. I miss the family I created too
  And the Christmas traditions
I carried on with them.

I feel the loss of my favorite store, with Naomi
  The place where I was known.
She knew what I liked
  In making my own special Christmas scene.
My home is full of the American crafts
  I found in her store,
The beautiful things people have made.

I remember the shock when I went to the store,
  Learning that they were closing,
But the reason was all the worse,

Their plans to move to California
        To be near grandchildren, thwarted
In the illness of her husband
        Who then died.
After the store was already being sold,
        With no return.

But even more,
        I feel the loss of the old family traditions
Of connection and excitement
        As we celebrated the Christmas season.
I lit the candle once more
        In memory of my mother
Remembering the Christmas traditions
        She began for us so long ago.
Despite all that,
        I feel a new kind of holiday sense evolving
Inside of me.

156

Valentine's Day Tradition

We went to Philadelphia to see Lois and Bill
     Once again marking our tradition
Of spending Valentine's Day weekend together.
     We still talk about the first—
Bill and Armin conspired
     With the arrangements
And we surprised Lois, walking into the restaurant.
     Even the waiters were in on the secret.

This year I had so much on my mind.
     I had emailed Lois with several agendas
To accomplish in our short time together.
     But the most important one
Was about our vacation.
     Armin had somehow avoided
Doing his homework
     And I had asked and reminded him
Repeatedly and then he said,
     "I don't think we can afford this trip
To Tuscany."

But Lois and I got on the internet
     With the resources she had collected
And began with rentvillas.com!
     By the end of the weekend,
Armin was engaged
     And has continued to do the research
To find us a special place.

He is already enraptured by reading
> Frances Mayes' *Under the Tuscan Sun*!
I am thrilled on many levels.
> Armin is functioning again,
Doing what he does best—
> Talking with people, making connections,
Creating something beautiful for us to enjoy
> And I don't have to do the work.

I love having something exciting
> To look forward to—
A new adventure, a beautiful place.
> I got Armin a book about Italian wineries
So he can choose some for us to visit.
> In spite of all the excitement of art
And Florence, inside, I imagine just resting—
> Luxuriating in the sun and Life.
I am happy.
> I feel the movement of New Life returning,
But different.
> As the impact of the illness fades for Armin
And the gains of confrontation and work bear fruit,
> I am hopeful about our life together.

I feel new energy and focus.
> I begin to weigh my use of time
As the valuable resource it is—
> To live well and lovingly
In the richness of the gifts we have
> And the purposes that seem important
To me.

Taking Stock

Armin left this morning for Florida
    For a weekend with his sister
And his brother who is also visiting.
    It felt nice that he was sad to leave me
With our newly emerging intimacy and comfort.

I am thrilled to have this time alone.
    Three and a half days with only my agenda.
My time at work is tense these days
    And I could relax and let go of the tension
In my gut, as I walked in the door last night
    At 11 pm—tense from the snowstorm
And driving through it.

 I went back to sleep when Armin left
    Took care of Junie when he barked,
Then slept until ten when my friend called.

I have written my Morning Pages
    Taking stock of where I am.
Somehow I have to get back the confidence
    In myself that I can handle what comes
With grace.

We have survived the year of cancer—
    I did get Armin through
The health care system.
    We made the best decision for his treatment,
Scary as it was,

Knowing that how and what we decided
        Could effect the outcome of his life.
I still remember with gratefulness,
        Sitting in the library with Ted
Our physician friend,
        Asking him to listen to the decision
And the facts that led us there,
        To be sure it all made sense
And I had not forgotten anything.
        Armin learned to manage his symptoms
Without flooding me with them,
        After I said I had had enough.

I did confront him with the issues between us—
        The part I couldn't change—
And he has begun to work on it—
        And to change.
The evidence of its usefulness
        Is in his feeling better
With more energy and direction
        About what he wants to do
Than he had before he got sick.

I am getting what I always wanted with him.
        He is kinder, more open,
Less willing to brush me off
        When he feels threatened.

Now, he wants to know when I am hurt—
        What it feels like to me now,

Instead of explaining it away
        With his good intentions or excuses.
Because of this,
        We get through our misunderstandings
More quickly now.

I like that and it feels good to me.
        We are even going
To a Marriage Encounter with Bruce and Elaine
        And will, in all likelihood,
Break all kinds of their rules.
        And we have a vacation to plan in Tuscany,
To look forward to with our friends, Lois and Bill.

So now it is my time to let go of the fear
        And take charge of the rest of my life.
With enough money,
        You can buy whatever you need, I think,
So it is just a matter of figuring out
        How to make money
From what I really want to do
        And get on with trusting myself to do that.
If I could do that at 17, I can surely do it now.
        I know that things are more complicated
Than I knew then.
        But I had already experienced a lot of life,
Triumphed in my own small ways
        And kept going
Even when I wasn't on top of it—yet.

So now I am at another crossroads
      And ready to move forward.
Eventually I will even be ready
      To work with my art again.
I picked up the phone to talk with Tom,
      My helpful attorney,
And said, "I am ready.
      I want you to negotiate
With the university for me
      For what I need in a buy-out."
And if I do not get it,
      I will just keep going
            With what I am doing,
Until I am finished.
      It will just take a bit longer.

"Let's go for it."

Seismic Shift

The letter arrived from the university today.
     Two and a half months after I sent a proposal
For a two year assignment of scholarly work
     Leading to my retirement,
Now, they have replied.

I had given up that they would respond.
     I had signed my appointment letter
For next year and negotiated my teaching schedule,
     Only this week learning
That something was afoot.

The letter indicated that the university
     Would respond positively to my proposal
In all of the substantial ways I requested—
     With the provision
That a satisfactory written legal document
     Will be reached.

I paused momentarily as I saw the source
     Of the letter
Which arrived in the morning mail
     In a house full of people.
I disappeared into myself to read it
     And then went to get Armin
To share it with him.
     It is hard to know or say how I feel.
But I sense a seismic shift has occurred
     In the underbelly structure of my existence,

Marking the moment of change
    Toward a new future
    Which I have been planning for
And evolving into
    For the past three and three-fourth years.

In my knowledge of the university
    And the skills from my past
I have used them on my own behalf
    To negotiate the terms of this transition
With the help of Tom, my attorney
    And the support of Armin in his love.

These past years have been tumultuous times
    For each of us,
Armin, recovering from his cancer
    And my own trauma.
But we have survived and grown—
    Exploring—
And creating new lives for ourselves.
    Even now a message from our attorney, Pat,
Tells us the State of New York has accepted
    The name of our new business entity,
The Center for Human Encouragement.
    Soon the final papers will arrive.

Gini was the first person I called.
    She said it felt freeing to her
That I might soon be in a clear place
    For moving into my future.

While I feel the seismic shift
    I cannot yet feel what it will bring.
I only know the deep rumbling of the plates,
    Making up the structure of my universe,
Have shifted today
    Toward some new definition of my future.

Flying West

I am touched and inspired
     By the play we saw last night,
Flying West by Pearl Cleage.
     Set in the town of Nicodemus, Kansas,
The state of my birth and growing-up,
     Strong African-American women
Fled Memphis for Kansas,
     Homesteading in a vision of freedom.
They went to Nicodemus
     Where everyone in that town for a while
Was Negro.

I am stirred in my Kansas roots again
     That Kansas was a free state.
But this history I had not known,
     That the place of Nicodemus could exist.

The strength of women homesteading touches me,
     Their holding on to valuable land.
Their vision of economic freedom rings inside,
     Making possible schools and libraries
And churches and families intact.

The relationships among these women
     Cross the generations,
Bringing healing to the injustices of slavery,
     Overcoming helplessness
With determination to prevail.

I come from a line of strong Kansas women.
      My grandmother left her West Virginia roots
And her mother and, as a school teacher,
      Traveled with her three brothers
To the Flint Hills of Kansas.
      I admire not only their courage,
But that of their mother who sent them
      To keep her sons out of the coal mines
Of West Virginia.

My grandmother married well
      And had four daughters.
Her young husband died suddenly of pneumonia,
      Leaving her with her fifth child,
A son, in her belly.
      Her in-law family
Robbed her of the comfortable life
      She had married into,
Claiming everything as theirs except for
      The small life insurance policy
Her husband had left for her alone.

My grandmother bought a house, a cow, chickens
      In the small town of Cedar Vale.
She clerked in a feedstore to support her children.
      She was even denied the support
      That would have allowed her
      To update her teaching certificate,
      Thus providing a more dignified life for her
      And for her family.

My mother grew up in that household
      And made her own dreams
For economic security.
      She took business courses in high school
To gain the skills to make her dream reality.
      While my father was the economic backbone
For our family in his work on the railroad,
      My mother worked most of her life,
Pausing only to bear her own five children.
      It was she who made things happen
For all of us.

My own dreams were born in my family,
      Nurtured by my parents' value for education.
My wishes for things I didn't have,
      But saw around me,
Fired my own determination
      To create a life for myself.
Though I was given much responsibility
      In my family,
Too soon in some ways,
      I took the things I had learned,
Knowing I could make things happen
      For myself.

My mother's entire salary for one year
      Launched the foundation
By paying for my college education.
      From there, I did the rest
With loans and work.

In some ways, my vision of empowerment,
    Evolving more consciously
In my life as a scholar,
    Grew out of that family
And my Kansas roots.

My daughters learned too of their heritage
    And lineage of strong Kansas women.
Each has created her own life
    Far from the Kansas prairie,
But close to these roots
    Of their foremother women.

Earlier I found and wrapped the videotapes
    About Susan B. Anthony
And Elizabeth Cady Stanton as birthday gifts
    For my granddaughters,
Katie and Molly at 12 and 13.
    They too will feel this widening circle
Of my roots.

No wonder I was so moved by the play!

* * * * * * * *

Postscript:
Now it is time to send the DVDs
    To Mairead and Caitrin, 13 and 10
As they make their own decisions
    About their future.

Storm

The wind is blowing fiercely,
  Shaking the trees in the sky
As if they will break or be uprooted
  By the force of the wind.

At first the sky was blue with white clouds moving
  Across the expanse of my skylights.
Now the sky is gray
  As if the storm is deepening.

A woman came to my door
  Asking for money to help her.
I know we are a target,
  Living in this big house.

I gave her the money she asked for
  Which was all I had in the house.
But then she asked me to drive her
  And I could not bring myself to go out.

My interior landscape is gray
  As the sky has become.
I had another round with Armin
  That feels as if my dream is vanishing.

I don't understand why this dream is so elusive
  When it is a dream we shared
From the beginning.

I imagine older people, some at least,
    Have found peacefulness in their shared life
Of long years even though I know
    That many just exist from habit,
Convenience, or lack of energy
    To change the status quo.

I think I will not find that intimacy in my lifetime
    And grieve for the lost dream.
In its place I reach deep inside
    And know it is up to me to choose
How I will live each moment of what remains.

Holding the Line

The small steps Armin is making
     Have begun to reverberate
Back into our relationship.
     After two weeks I cautiously acknowledge
That I am experiencing his changes—
     But that I remain guarded
About my vulnerability.

Armin surges ahead in his enthusiasm
     Telling me six times in two days
How much he loves me.
     But I am so tense, my jaws locked
I will not buy into his fantasy world.

I am still angry and hurt
     That he does not hear me
Or take seriously what I say to him.
     He "forgot" that he agreed to apologize
To Jerry about involving him
     In our private matters.
I was left seething for two hours,
     While they avoided our encounter and
Armin ran his enthusiasm about the bouillabaisse
     He was making for dinner.

Finally in my sleeping seething I remembered
     That I agreed to have Jerry come
Only when Armin agreed to apologize
     And I would not have to bear alone

The responsibility of picking up the pieces
        From that fateful encounter.
I confronted Armin and he laughed
        About his forgetting—
And went ahead with his apology.
        But he presented it so lightly
That Jerry demurred in accepting it
        Until I filled in the meaning.
It was the first time I had seen Armin
        Be so casual with another,
His best friend, Jerry,
        In a matter of conflict.

For all these years I struggled
        That it was something about me
That let Armin treat me so painfully
        Without even hearing me.
Even when I told him directly of my pain,
        He did not respond,
Or open his process to me.

This encounter was about going to the Forum
        In Japan. He was still recovering
From his radiation treatment for the cancer.
        I was still struggling with my feelings
Of aloneness and abandonment
        Through it all.
I went to the Iowa Summer Writing Program
        With my friend, Jeanne.
I remember the moment
        When I got off the phone with Armin.

173

He told me that he was going to go with me.
　　　　I told Jeanne,
"I guess I am going to have a life again."
　　　　Jerry had been visiting Armin
While I was gone.
　　　　When I got home I learned
That Armin had discussed the issue with Jerry
　　　　And had decided not to go.
I was hurt that he was not going,
　　　　But furious, that he had involved Jerry
In such a private matter between us
　　　　Especially after all we had been through
With his cancer.

Finally I put the pieces together in another way
　　　　That he does not take seriously
What I say to him about how I feel
　　　　When it involves HIM!

Many years ago I listened,
　　　　While we were attending the Forum
In England, just two years after we met.
　　　　He and Nat and Jerry,
The Trio, gifted psychologists each
　　　　And friends of many years
Were making a presentation about their work,
　　　　Listening and being with clients.
Armin was eloquent—
　　　　A part of my knowing—
That he is a gifted therapist.

But in that room I could not contain myself.
	I burst into tears and ran out of the room
Trying to shield my vulnerability from others
	In my pain.
I said to him then
	That I hurt so much.
My pain was that he did not treat me
	In any way with the care he gave
To his clients.
	None of the three of them could hear
And looked at me so strangely.

Now all these years later,
	It is finally getting clear to me
The lengths Armin will go
	To avoid any sense of conflict
If it is about anything in our relationship.

Mining

A man once asked me, in a business context,
    What I do when I get myself
In a difficult place with my work.
    He had observed something,
I no longer remember what,
    That I was having trouble with.
I just dig myself out, I replied, *And go on.*

On the surface of things,
    This is what I have been doing
These past years,
    Digging myself out of the biggest mess
I have ever been in in my working life.
    But, as I look more deeply, I realize
I have turned my attention not to digging out,
    But to mining.

Inside myself I have mined,
    Looking for how to save my life
From these assaults.
    But what I found was
Gold and silver and sapphires and opals,
    All jewels that I love.

I have found them inside of me,
    Waiting to be discovered.
Layer after layer, new paths have emerged—
    Some dead ends, some monumental threats,
Like Armin's illness.

Sometimes I have crawled,
Barely able to put one foot in front of the other.
     But I have kept moving.

I have found leads in the newspaper,
     In the world around me.
I have found company and support
     From fellow miners,
Each looking in our own ways.

I am not finished yet with mining—
     Perhaps I never again will be.
But I have a stockpile of jewels
     Discovered, waiting
To be woven into the fabric
     Of my New Life.

I am trying once again
     To trust the process of these small steps
Unfolding inside of me.
     I discovered them early in this crisis
And slowly, step-by-step
     They led me to a new life
Of hope and joy and creativity.

I have followed Julia's path of discovery,
     The Artist's Way.
Writing Morning Pages clears my mind
     And sometimes becomes the poem
Written to explore my experience
     And feelings of my journey.

My Studio

The third floor in our old house
      Was servants' quarters in some earlier time.
It was three rooms and a bath with low ceilings
      But dark with dormer windows.

Meg and John had lived there
      In the recycling process of home and college
But soon they were gone
      And it was empty for a long time.

I imagined doing something with it
      But my imagination was lit
The day Gerry and I looked above the opening
      In the closet ceiling—
To see 9 feet at the peak!
      My imagination took off.

It was a long and scary process to build my studio.
      But with the talents of Bill, the architect
And Gerry ,the master carpenter, and his crew
      It became a glorious space—
With a lot of money spent in the process.

My condo furniture came home from storage
      Where our friend Bruce had kept it for me.

My studio has never again looked as pristine
      As in the photographs.
A lot of "stuff" came—

To be sorted, filed—and junked!
    But it is a working studio.

I actually learned to use my computer—
    Now with double screens—
Space for thousands of photo slides
    The easel and painting supplies
With storage for framed art
    And endless photographs
That never made it into albums,
    But some eventually finding a home
In my books
    And on my walls.

The fireplace is my favorite for winter reading
    With instant heat and beautiful flame.

Family and friends have found
    A comfortable place to stay—
For visits—or longer in some situations.

Despite Armin's fears,
    I continued to come down
To live with him!

And he got a beautiful new shower
    For his patience.

But it fulfills its purpose and I am delighted—
    It is a working studio!

My Garden

My garden is my palette
    The flowers my paints.
I choose the plants with spontaneity—
    The color, shape and blooms entice.
With Milli's help we place them,
    In the space where they will thrive.

In my back garden two yews are left
    And a huge old maple tree
Here when I came—the maple now near its end.
    And a gorgeous deep purple magenta
Tree peony which has bloomed every year.
    I have no idea how old it is.
I have added tree peonies
    Of beautiful colors to keep it company
And the most unusual one, named
    Gaughan which Milli took a piece of
When our neighbors moved away.

In the front garden
    There is a large pink dogwood
And a cherry tree here when I came.
    I knew I loved pink dogwoods
From the one I planted at my home
    In Arlington, which my father
Pruned—when he was visiting,
    Much to my dismay.

There were five old tall evergreen trees
    One of which dropped sap on our cars,
Much to our annoyance.
    We cut it down and were so delighted
With the light it let in,
    We took down the rest.

I had one design proposal for landscaping
    And hated it—
When came a knock.
    Milli was working
On the garden next door
    And came to ask about the boundary.
I answered her question
    And then it registered
        Perennial Designs—
And went to talk with her.
    A friendship was born
From the front garden we created together—
    And the expansion and care
Over the years.

Our friendship survived and thrived
  Just like my garden—
Because she has a tolerance
  For my bringing home new plants
And then saying, "Milli, where will these go?"

And then there were the curly willow trees
  Lining one side in the back.
We got tired of the mess they made
Even when we pruned them back severely
  And finally said,"Enough!"
Now there are two flowering pear trees
  White blossoms
Reaching for the sky in early spring,
  Pink and white dogwoods
And a maple marking the boundary
  On one side of our back yard,
A lovely Japanese maple on another side.
  With the redwood fence,
  The trees create a private secluded garden
  In the midst of the city.

My favorite trees are the Prairie Fire crabapple
  Along the porch in front
Another in the back.
  I love their flowing free-form shape
And the beautiful blossoms
  Of bright magenta.

There is one amazing flower in the back.
    A hibiscus grew way beyond expectations
Producing bright red flowers as big as a plate
    More than twenty blooms at once.
Though the flowers last only a day,
    The blossoms continue in late summer!

Along the back fence we had drama.
        One huge alianthus tree, a volunteer,
Had planted itself beyond the fence and uprooted
        Crashing through the fence,
Damaging the first of the tulip trees.
        That lined the back.
When another uprooted we removed the other two.
        A beautiful maple,
        The Prairie Fire,
A tulip magnolia and viburnum took their place
        Each bringing blossoms in spring
Or the changing colors of the maple in fall.

On a different note,
        I have a "thing" about hydrangeas.
There were some left in the front
        That turn magenta in the fall.
And then we went to Nantucket and discovered
        Beautiful blue lace-cap hydrangeas.
Armin bought one for me
At the florist, Arena's, for some special day
        And we planted it right in the front.
It grew very large
        Staking its place in a prominent space
Blooming year after year.

For a long time I avoided planting lilacs
        When Armin said he was allergic to them.
But I tried Miss Kim and nothing happened
        So now I have several lilacs which I love,
Especially the deep purple and magenta ones.

187

The hanging baskets decorate the porch.
    Each year I try new things to see what works.
The pots line the steps to the porch
    Overflowing with lilac petunias
Reminding me of my friend, Tess, in Wales,
    Who had them inside her house!
This year I did not find the lilac petunias
    But the pots were overflowing in purple!

The pots in back began
    With four large hypertufa pots I had made
And then I discovered the beautiful blue ones
    Which also stand the Rochester winters.
I have a whole collection of them!
    I edged a way from blue to a huge green one
And planted, you guessed it,
    A beautiful white hydrangea.

When I saw the gorgeous fields of lavender
    In Provence,
The lavender became a new addition to my garden.

If you have read all of this,
    You know I love my garden!
A pink dogwood and a pussywillow
    Remember my father.
The pansies and peonies
    First came from my mother.
The pansies, her favorite,
    Became a tradition,
    To mark the beginning of spring.

The Buddha in the back,
        Just beyond the pool
Was a housewarming gift to Armin
        From his friends, Nat and Jerry.
We began with lighting it
        And expanded
To lighting the rimming of the garden
        At night.

I found oriental lanterns
        From the shop of OckHee's,
Who also became a friend.
        Over many years I looked
For a sculpture to remember Jeanine
        And found "Fairy" at OckHee's.
She is beautiful at night in the lights
        As well as in the day.

My garden is magical at night—
    From my upstairs window
I look out to enjoy the lights
    Bringing a sense of comfort
And peace—since Armin died.

When Junie Too came on New Year's Eve
    I made many trips to the backyard
At night
    And discovered the magic
In the winter sky
    And the lights of my garden.
It helped to offset the pain
    Of being awakened
In the middle of the night to take him out!

In the beginning
    I enjoyed the work of my garden.
I have had Milli's help to maintain it
    As well as that of her helpers.
I have a finger, crooked from arthritis
    Before I discovered
It is not a tool to clean the weeds!

Much of the garden is stable now—
    Full to overflowing at times
And I am glad to have help to care for it
    In the changing seasons.
I still enjoy designing
    And planting my pots and baskets
As each spring brings new energy.

Each year, as spring arrived,
    Armin and I moved our meals
To the backporch
    To enjoy our private world
Overlooking the pool and my garden.
    He was ingenious in discovering
Ways to attract the flies and other insects
    Elsewhere.
And we could enjoy our meals
    Without visitors!
It was the place where Armin still sat
    Even in his wheelchair
        As his life was ebbing.

There is a burial place in my garden
    Where each of our dogs has a marker—
A red heart and their name on a stone
    Ellie, Annie, Francie and Junie
To remember them
    The special place they hold
In our shared lives
    And in our heart.

Sometimes I think my garden will be
    The resting place for our ashes too
This special place of home and garden
    I shared with Armin
    From my first visit—to the end—
    A place of deep love, connection
    And beauty.

Gratitude

Since this year began—
    And with it a new millennium
I have read each day
    <u>Simple Abundance</u> about comfort and joy.
I first heard about it when Jo gave it to my Mother
    And said she could have written it.
    I found it and was drawn to it—
    This somewhat connection with my mother.

Some days the thoughts strike a deep chord within.
    Others they are just pleasant to think about.
I began to not only read the book each day
    But think about
The changes I am making in my life.
    And write them in a Journal of Gratitude.

The simple act of increasing my awareness
    Of gratitude for the parts of my life
Which are gifts and the people I value
    Provides a few moments to reflect.
And I experience peacefulness.

In this time of loss
    I feel grateful for the riches I have
Which I can use to guide me
    In this search for my dreams.
And in its presence, I am grateful for my life,
    Despite its current difficulties.

Body

My mind searches while my body betrays me.
    The leftovers from disappointments
In my life hang onto every cell,
    Burdening me with weight
And muscles grown soft through lack of use.

Take charge! I hear the scream
    From deep inside.
I have ignored it for so long it is as if
    I had silenced the voice of my own being.

You're looking at so much,
    Why not me?
What keeps you from seeing
    That I need your attention too.
Mind and spirit—yes.
    But what about body?
You cannot exist without me.
    Why do you ignore
What sits in front of you
    Each time you look in the mirror?

It isn't just age but inactivity
    Buried under layers designed to silence
The voice that speaks to you,
    Even screams at you.

Get with it—as with your other agendas.
    Find balance and connection

Within your body
	Before you go looking
For lofty, higher goals.

If you don't, I will claim my due
	And neither of us will be happy
With what it took to finally gain
	Your attention.

If we ever do.

First Steps Back

The sense of responsibility I took on again
    When Armin got sick
Feels like a vise around my chest,
    Restricting my breath
And squeezing the Life Force out of me.

It is only now that he is almost well,
    With renewed energy,
And friends commenting how well he looks,
    That I can really pay attention
To what happened to me.

Armin is excited by his new found discoveries
    Of himself.
He is ready to move forward in his work
    With people going through
This cancer experience.
    I am clear I want to be a part of this
And want spouses' experiences
    To find a voice and be heard.

We met with Teri to take the first steps,
    Leading to this new adventure.
It feels good that we are finally creating
    A dream we had so many years ago—
The Center for Human Encouragement.
    We are together.
Armin's new changes are leading
    To a new landscape between us.

But I am aware of my closedness
And continuing sadness.
The responsibility about his cancer
And his needs
For me to be there with him,
Have lifted in the outer world
But remain inside of me.
I face the reality that the aftermath
Of all of this is still with me.

The difficulties we have had in our relationship
Through all these years
Are shifting as Armin gives up his protections
And negotiated mindset
For a more open, flowing space between us.

But I am like a muscle, long unused,
Atrophied behind the shell I use
To protect myself.
I still have the wish for openness
But hide my vulnerability in ways I've used
All these years.

But then I face the worst part—
I had been creating a new more free life.
For the first time, relieved of a lifelong
Cloak of responsibility,
I was out there, creating in words
In paint and photography,
Exploring new ways to express my self,
Creating a new life.

The blow of losing that
        Was like the light going out
Inside of me.

The effort to relight the process seems
        Overwhelming.
I can see what I lost, but somehow seem
        Unable to grieve for it
Or feel that the path is once again open to me.

I started a month ago
        To again write Morning Pages
But find it hard to do regularly.
        I began again at the beginning to read
The Artist's Way
        But can't get beyond the first chapter
Of creating a sense of safety.

I do not feel safe in opening myself again
        To this life-creating process.
I am frightened at a deep level
        That were I to try again,
I could not sustain another loss—
        There have been too many losses.

And yet, this place I am in is a negative,
        Downward spiraling process.
I can not stay here without everything
        Unraveling to nothing.

At my better times,
 I have tackled the next steps
And tried to accept my thinking as having merit
 For my future.

But I really do not know which way to turn.
 I have made progress
In ordering my studio—
 Tiny steps that extend the span of order
Over chaos
 To the work I want to do.
I don't know.
 Can I write my way through this morass?
Make a list of next steps to do
 And see if moving these tiny steps
Will finally lead me to real work for my future
 And openness once more inside of me.

Another Step

We went to see our accountant
    To get more advice for moving our dream
Forward.
    He was very helpful in sending us
To see our attorney
    To set up the Center's structure
And now suggests that we open
    A separate bank account.

I made an appointment to get advice
    About my retirement assets
And took another step in the direction
    To move ahead.
I am frightened what this can mean
    But it is clear I want to know
So that I can plan my strategy and timetable.
    It is still January
And we can start the new year
    With this new dream.

I sent off an email to Tess
    To explore how we can be together
In the summer.
    I began to shift my perspective
From conflicts in my schedule
    To inclusiveness and openness
In ways to work together with my friends.
    This feels like a new way of being
In my world.

Between us, Armin and I have begun a dance
        Of quiet, gentle movements
With each other,
        Exploring his new openness
And my protective inching
        Out of my hiding place.

I must find out slowly
        Whether this intimate world between us
Is now safe for my openness
        And hope for our dreams
As it was in the beginning.

AN EARLY HAPPY TIME

Healing

The process of healing with Armin
      Goes on very slowly.
Yet it is a consistent presence
      When before
It wasn't even on the horizon.
      Only my intermittent blow-ups
Reveal the underlying pain
      Without hope of its resolution.

I think of the past year
      And see the currents flowing
And converging
      In the horrific explosions that happened
When I connected with my pain.

At first there was fear of Armin's diagnosis
      With a life-threatening illness.
We struggled through informing ourselves
      And the decisions about treatment
Which would effect his life.
      I was helpful
In getting the medical opinions
      And weighing the risks
Of one against the another.
      But in the end it was only Armin and I
And those who love him
      Who will bear the impact
         Of our decisions.

I felt Armin's abandonment of me
  As he disappeared into his focus
On himself, determined to continue working
  As he endured the fear of the treatments
And their after effects.
  All the while he felt and acknowledged
My presence and support
  But could not hear my loss
Of his company.

Just when we thought we had made it through
  And celebrated the end of treatments
The fatigue set in and got progressively worse.
  It was the hardest time, we thought,
Until the convergence of the currents.

I remember still the sequence
  Leading up to the moment
I heard Jerry say that Armin had discussed
  With him his reluctance to go to Japan
Before he had shared it with me.

The explosion in my gut was of the violation
  I felt of the private world we shared.
Suddenly all of the pain, the unresolved pain,
  Of our nineteen years together
Was present in my anguish and screaming.

The pain could no longer be ignored
  Nor would gradual dissipation hide it—
Again.

Only confronting it was an option
　　　As I began to speak with Armin
About my determination that he face
　　　The long-buried pain in him
That kept us apart
　　　From the intimacy I craved,
As did he.

I felt the fear and risk of losing everything.
　　　Knowing that relationships
Sometimes do not survive
　　　Such life-threatening illness
Only increased my terror.
　　　But I also knew that deep exploration
Of one's self could be a part
　　　Of the healing process.

I insisted Armin talk with Gini
　　　And be open
To her psychophysiological nursing expertise.
　　　I no longer trusted his explorations
With the friends with whom he had shared
　　　So much of his life.
Gini's visit to see me at a crucial time was for her.
　　　But it became a turning point for Armin.
I still remember, sitting in the library
　　　As she showed him with her arms
The energy that could not get through his body.

They talked several times before she left
　　　And regularly after that by telephone.

After each call I recognized,
    As he shared with me some of it,
That he was talking with her about serious matters.
    Gradually I began to experience
The changes in him.
    But I held out, wondering if they would effect
The relationship between us.
    Slowly I began to notice
That he was different with me.
    But I remained cautious
    In my closed and isolated world.

****

I learned the pieces of Armin's story in small segments over the years. His first comment that his mother did not love him seemed strange, especially when later his brother Robert said, "He was her favorite." It was not only the pain between us, but my recognition, finally, that Armin had a lot of grief from those early experiences in his family, grief that I knew. I said he must talk with Gini, our colleague of many years because I knew she would not let him avoid or escape the feelings that he had held inside all those years.

My First Love
My First Friend

I've been missing you so much for seventy years!
I have felt so much pain about losing you.
You were my foster mother for my first five years,
      Loving, nurturing, constantly encouraging,
      And modeling, sharing an open way of being.
We were intimate friends, as I wish were all
      Parents and children.
You helped me live with the rest of the family,
But I felt that open way of being
      And closeness only with you.
My other mother kept her distance—
      Until she began
      Screaming her jealousy of our love
      And my father's love for you.
You screamed your pain as she sent you away.
Our family exploded!
My father was in and out of our home
      For the next three years.
I felt terrified, helpless, and all alone.
It was a death.

Twenty years ago, you reentered my life in a
      Gracious form.
But after living a half century in the ruins of a
      Broken world,
      Despite much rebuilding
      And recreating on my part,

I was still covered up, and almost blind
    To that deeply open way of being.
My broken world had tutored me
    Destructively—and,
I couldn't recognize you!

You tried to tell me who you were,
    But our worlds clashed.
From my broken world,
    I did not understand.
All I knew was our tenderness,
    And that I loved you tremendously.
You kept challenging me
    To open up more and more.
I did, slowly, without understanding you,
    Or recognizing you.
In our most recent clash,
    You bespoke brilliantly!
And I heard you fully!
I felt a huge breakthrough
    Into a very deep, un-defensive openness.
It shocked me into an enormous sadness.

My sadness spoke
    Of all our misunderstandings
    And pain over our twenty years,
    Separate from
    Our many times of happiness.
I was, and am, grieving, mourning deeply.

I feel a strange relief,
    With joy
    And overwhelming sadness together.
I know that I can not go back—
    And now I want even more.

I want to be
    My deepest childhood openness.
I want to be that openness with you.

    Armin Klein
    February, 2003

Convergence

I asked Armin to listen to me in the library
    When I finally realized
I could not find the connection
    With my feelings which lay so close
Yet beneath the surface of my awareness.

I reviewed the gains of the past months
    Looking for the clue,
The door of my entry inward.
    Armin's regaining energy and strength
I am glad for
    But I do not feel better.
His changes from this work with Gini,
    I recognize
But I do not feel better.
    The impact of those changes
In our relationship, I see
    But I do not feel better.

I circled around myself
    Until I saw I was swimming in the moat
Surrounding the castle
    Behind whose walls of stone
My feelings lay.
    The image made it all concrete.

In my class that night I showed the film
    Of Living in the Light of Death—
Bill Bartholome's story of his discovery of cancer

And the heightened awareness
　　He experienced of the joys of living
As he faced his end.
　　I heard his wife speak my own words
Of her invisibility and isolation
　　When no one asked,
"What is it like for you?"
　　As her world crumbled as surely
As each pound her husband lost,
　　Becoming a skeleton that he said
Would survive his death.
　　The rumbling inside of me
Shook the walls of my castle shell.

The next morning Jeanne called,
　　Responding to a note I had sent her.
I had recalled and shared with her
　　The liveliness we had known
In our Iowa writing sojourn,
　　The loss when we returned home
To injury and responsibility with our husbands.
　　I was deeply touched
By our reconnecting.

That night, alone with just Armin and Jeanne
　　I began to share and explore
The dimensions of my grief,
　　Coming into awareness as I entered
The castle door,
　　Having found the way inside.

I roamed freely within my grief
        Past and present and future
All a part of my losses, my fears
        For my and our future.

I feel abandoned by Armin
        As I move through the rooms of my grief.
His silence feels so familiar
        Like the talk about everything
Around the table of my childhood family home
        Covering over the feelings that lay within.

I yelled at Armin in my frustration
        And he disappeared into his cave,
Abandoning me completely.
        My despair becomes so powerful
And pervasive
        I have no connection with hope
That anything between us will ever change.
        I fear that he will sicken and die
Or will I,
        Without the intimacy we long for
And imagined possible when we met.

In my half-waking state
        I told him I feel forced back into my cave
By the lashing he does with his feelings
        When he is terrified.
Somehow he hears my graphic description
        And feels its resonance within himself.
Things begin to move between us

As words give voice to feelings
        Of the events we shared.

In the night, Armin began to talk
        And I challenged him on his hiding
Behind his role and fear within the group.
        He actually hears and begins to imagine
How he will go further with them
        When I am not there.

Still he makes no move back to the experience
        I shared with him
And the place where our rupture occurred.
        I insist we return to the solid ground
Of those events
        Instead of the wandering around
He does inside his head,
        Thinking I can read his mind
(Which I have told him many times
        I am unable to do).

I am finally moving through my loss and grief—
        The loss of Jeanine,
Armin tells me of his memory
        The first time I shared it with him.
The scattered crumbs I have dropped
        Over the years,
He repeats them all, making it clear
        He has heard me and felt for me
But could not tell me directly.
        It is also clear that my losses link with his

But it is only in the wracking cough
    I hear from him now
That I know he is in his own unexplored
    Grief.

I circled around
    The early loss of my mother,
The pieced together fragments,
    That brought me to the clear link
That my father had become my mother
    In my infancy.
I remembered our reuniting finally
    When my feelings erupted,
"I want to be with you, Mom,"
    And the peacefulness it brought to her
When I told her
    I would be with her to the end.

I remembered being led away
    By my brother-in-law
When I had done all there was for her body,
    But wanting really to stay
And be with her
    In those last ending moments of her life.

I remembered sitting beside her on the bed,
    Playing the music
That Cindy and I
    Had gotten for her,
Trying to sing the hymns through my grief.
    I remembered her singing too

Despite the drugs that overpowered
    Her conscious awareness.
I still feel the shock and anger in my gut
    When Jim shut off the music
Claiming it was time for her medicine.
    My feeble argument
That the music together was medicine
    Came not even close
To his protective feelings for her
    That hid his own pain of loss.

Through the rooms of the castle I traveled,
    Remembering my urgent visit to Jean
After all the years of my loss of her.
    I cannot believe I left behind
My four week old baby in her father's care—
    So great was my wish and need
To reconnect the one loss that was retrievable.

I gave voice to my anger with my brother, Jim,
    Who said back to me
That even with Dad in the nursing home,
    I would still be saying,
"It doesn't have to be this way."
    But Dad still knew me
In the nursing home
    And I could be alone with him
In the love and connection we had shared
    From my infancy to his death—

And I knew
        That I had been able to give back to him
All that he had given to me.
        Through my vigil with him,
Acting on his behalf, When he
        Could no longer speak for himself,
        I helped to carry out the wishes
He had been clear about,
        His wishes for his life.

And then the sharing of events,
        The memorial for Mother in the Arboretum
And finally the remembrance of Jeanine,
        This place of beauty and life
Helped to make the connection
        That our family loss
Had also been a loss to others
        In our community.

Finally I had shared it all with Armin
        And he had not only heard
But been a part of it as well
        And listened as I put it all together
In healing for myself.

Instead of one loss, I begin to feel
        The loss of wasted time—
And wonder why it took me so long
        To recognize these powerful forces
Inside of me.

I feel humbled by my riches
  Of love and feelings and images of beauty
  And the opportunities before me.

* * * * * * * * *

After Armin's death, I found a newer poem which I do not remember having seen before. In it, he wrote of every thing I had shared with him over the years about Jeanine's death and how I had been affected by it. He also shared his vision that she had been a part of our shared life together all these years.

I was moved and comforted in my loss of him that he had heard me and been with me in my loss.

JEANINE'S MEMORIAL
PARSONS, KANSAS ARBORETUM

A Beautiful Day

Before I was even out of bed this morning
    Armin called from Georgia
With a special message of love
    From his nighttime dreaming.
What a nice way to start the day.

Soon I was working on a project
    Juggling time to complete it
Before the secretary left on vacation
    And I would have to stop
For an important meeting.

When the telephone rang, I was expecting Gini
    For our weekly connecting
And supporting.
    But I was surprised when it was Cindy,
My youngest daughter.
    Usually she is at work at that hour.
We caught up on the outcome
    Of her latest challenge at work
And then she told me her news.

I held my breath waiting
    As she told me she is pregnant.
I am so happy and excited for her and Keith—
    And for myself, that she has included me
In this wonderful news.
    I know to be cautious so early
But my joy refuses to be squelched!

I finished my work and faxed it off,
    Wishing the secretary a happy vacation
And dashed off to my meeting with the lawyer
    Who will help us
With setting up our center.

An hour and a half later, he looked at his watch
    And said, "It's 2:30. I could have
An entity for you by 5 o'clock.
    Suddenly I knew that what we want
Is possible and a whole new world lay ahead
    On my terms.

But the day was not yet over.
    Janet and I met to tackle
The Medical Center Library
    To see if we could extract articles
On empowerment for my writing.
    The technology might have defeated me
Alone, even though I got there in time
    To ask for help.
But together we hit the jackpot.
    I quit when I was too embarrassed
To continue what we weren't really authorized
    To do, but we had enough to feel good
And begin to take the next step.

And still, there was more to come.
    My friend, Jackie,
Was having surgery today
    Determined to correct a problem

Instead of just living with
    Someone's mistake.
When I returned home I learned
    She had come through the surgery well.
I was very touched and relieved to hear.

Just last night Thomas asked
    If anything good was happening
Amid the negative stuff.
    The coming meeting was the only thing
I could say was good.

One evening later I couldn't stop talking
    With Armin. For an hour
I went on and on, sharing the wonderful things
    That happened today.
It was the last gift, deeply felt,
    To be able to feel his joy and love
That I have had this Beautiful Day.

The Light

I can only live in the moment
    As I travel this new path.
When I try to talk about the past
    Or think about the future,
I am lost in the anger, confusion and blame
    And vow not to be open
Or share anything
    About either past or future.

But sometimes I can find the place
    Deep inside myself where peace resides.
I feel myself as part of the universe
    Unfolding in its own time and way,
Without the effort and determination
    With which I have always lived my life—
As if I alone
    Must and could control my universe.

When I am in that peaceful place
    The world is rich in its gifts.
People enter who help me find my next steps
    Or open doors
Through which my creative spirit
    Finds its way to new places
Connecting with all kinds of spirits
    And possibilities.
I love myself in that open space
    And I am filled with love
For those around me

Also finding their ways—
        Young and old;
Those still here and those already gone
        Are here for me in ways I never imagined
But now seem quite natural.

I am filled with gratitude for these riches
        That bring such joy
And hopefulness to my life
        And wonder why it took so long
For me to see the light.

My only wish—
        I might have found my way here sooner.

Shared Space

I want to be free in this space we share
      Living together between you and me.
I have controlled so many of my feelings
      Carrying around the tension
And pain of it all in my neck.

I have worked gradually all these years
      To try to diminish my headaches and pain
Which come from controlling my experience
      In the worlds I lived in—
To protect myself from the attacks of others.

It is hard to be a visionary
      To see possibilities not seen by others
And to withstand their reactions
      Of threat under the cloak of reason—
It isn't feasible, practical or wanted.

Suddenly I was cast out of my world of work
      The scope narrowed—
To the classes I teach.
      But in the process my world has opened
Wider to new possibilities.

I have learned some things by all of this.
      I want to work alone
And with people I like
      Enjoying my work, protecting it
And myself from so many attacks.

I am wise enough to know that not all people
        Will agree, but I believe I can create
A playing field where agreements can be made,
        Explicitly,
And changed when they no longer fit
        For me or for them.

I am learning to protect my artist self
        In ways I never understood before,
Leaving myself open to vulnerability and pain.

In my most private world with Armin
        I have withheld some of my openness
As well, some of it
        Because of what I experience
In our interactions,
        Some of it because I could not manage
The breadth and depth of the canyon
        Between my world of work
And world at home with him.

And now the space seems very tight
        And I am caught between the vise
My wish for freedom for myself
        His reactions to me
When I am not controlled.

I cannot avoid hurting him
        Not all his scars are mine.
He brings a lifetime of hurts and scars
        And so do I.

He saw that when he called us
     "Battle-scarred veterans"
When we married.

My hope is that somehow we will find the ways
     To be gentle with our hearts
Without creating pain for each other.
     I know that love is not enough
I have been down that path before.

We must find the words
     That express our feelings
And with them create a wider opening space
     To live within together.

Four Years

It was four years ago my mind reminds,
    Awakening me from my sleep
And fitful dreams.
    The stones are lined up on the window sill
To mark the passage of time
    Lest I forget.

We were on vacation in Nantucket
    Enjoying the escape and summer beach
With our dear friends, and fellow adventurers,
    Lois and Bill.
My anxiety about my work was high,
    Knowing
That something terrible was coming.
    But mostly I was able to leave it behind
In the beautiful weather
    And space of Nantucket.

We rode our bicycles to the beach—
    It was a **long** ride for city dwellers
And it was fun.
    We celebrated a special dinner
At Chanticleer
    And took pictures
Of the famous carousel horse
    Who went exploring
In the middle of the night,
    Making that part
Of Nantucket lore famous

In a children's book I love.
(I brought home copies for my grandchildren.)

I remember the phone call
    That ended my vacation.
The Vice-Chancellor to whom I reported
    In my work called to tell me
There would be an unwelcome article
    In the newspaper about my school.
Students, feeling angry,
    That they had been deceived,
Got a lawyer and then a reporter
    To tell their story, taking seriously
The empowerment I had so often shared
    With them.

I still can feel the tension of that call in my gut
    As memory returns,

But was it really necessary for me to be called
    When I was on vacation
When there was nothing he said
    He wanted me to do?
Cruelty, perhaps.

Today we arrived in Tuscany
    To share a home for two weeks,
Once again with our friends, Lois and Bill,
    And Armin and me.
Perhaps that is the connection
    That brings back the earlier memory.

The four years have been momentous ones
    For each of us
And all of us are at new places in our lives.
Bill has made the most dramatic change,
    Leaving a job of many years
As an architect with the State Department
    To become a full time art student
    Along with his work as an architect.
We have marked his progress in many ways
    Watching his work emerge,
Sometimes even being the subjects of his art—
    One famous one, a woodcut print,
Taken from an old photograph of me at seventeen,
    Projecting me into my future.
"Queen of the Universe," he called it!

Armin has endured his round of cancer
    And probed deeply his lifelong scars

And pain which has helped us move
        To a deeper place in our relationship.
I am happy for that and we are grateful
        To be beyond the cancer.

Lois is in the midst of her own transition
        Completing a book
About the important work she led
        Demonstrating nursing excellence
In a world of faculty practice
        Too many leave behind.

And I—
        Rocked by the pain of loss and blame,
The poetry I had seldom written
        Flows freely now to document
The times and places of my life.
        I have a beautiful studio for my work
Which Bill designed and helped me realize.
        My painful detour during Armin's cancer
Brought new strains, but clarification
        About the path I wish to follow
In charting my own way.

The university has said
        That soon it will give its agreement
To a plan I have proposed
        And I will move into my own work
For two years leading to my retirement.
        By then I hope to have written
About my work on empowerment

While I have empowered myself
    Through my own transition.
I hope too that our new
    Center for Human Encouragement
Will be a thriving reality.

I feel peaceful
    In the new intimacy I share with Armin
Even happy
    Now that my dreams are being realized
In this closeness we share.

"What is this overwhelming tenderness?"
    Armin wrote, now twenty years ago.

I feel its presence inside me in a new way
    As we move into this beautiful dream
Of being together in Tuscany.

Four years ago I said
    My garden
Would be beautiful in the spring.

My garden is beautiful
    And so is my life and our friendships
And our love.

Happy Anniversary, My Love!

Today we have been married
>for twenty years!
At our age and time of life, it is the same as
>fifty years in the lives of young folks.
We will have to live a long time to catch up.
>>In one more year, our marriage will reach
>>the adulthood of twenty one years.
We will have to be serious and mature,
>no more humor and fun.
So this will be our last year to frolic.
>>We will have to settle down and stop laughing,
>>stop our amusement at human foibles,
Human superstitions, human "knoeledge,"
>and human faith
In an arrogantly anthropormorfic,
>`   human invented god.
We will have to admit that we do know
>that there is no wisdom,
That there is no knowledge
>related to the human spirit,
Only to human, concrete, technical progress,
>>which mechanical model we try to apply
>>to the mysterious unmechanical human
>>spirit,
The drive for growth!

Let us hope that the adultness of our marriage
>will help me accept
That there are no guide lines for human existence,

That there is nothing on which to rely except love,
    and that with love
There must be its partners; misunderstanding
    and anger.
I hope that I will be able to learn
    during this twenty first year
To give you an anniversary gift of my comfort
    with those partners.

For twenty years,
    I have hoped to do away with anger.
It is only now that I am beginning to see
    that anger is
A misunderstood part
    of the growth drive of love.

                Armin Klein
                August 20, 2003

234

Away in Tuscany

We have rented a house in Tuscany
      For our two weeks of vacation.
Found via email and pictures on the internet,
      It is a house that has stood
In the same place for many years.
      It is halfway or more up the mountain
From the town of Camoire.

We are comfortable in our house
      With the changes made
To adapt to modern times—somewhat.
      Yet we are isolated too
Without a telephone
      And even the cellphone does not work
Surrounded by the mountains.

Slowly we settle into a different pace of life.
      I have my clock completely turned around
Having traveled from California to New York
      To Tuscany in less than a week's time.
I am awake at night, reading and writing
      And sleep long stretches from exhaustion
As I find myself in this new place.

Just going to the market
      Is an anxious adventure at first
Since all together we know very little Italian.
      The storm arrived this morning
With loud thunder and bolts of lighting.

Mara, the wife of the grounds keeper,
    Arrived to reassure us
    That the house is safe
And how to turn the electricity back on
    When it goes off.

I mostly slept through the storm
    Enjoying the cool weather and breeze
Compared with the heat of yesterday.
    Each day we talk about getting organized
To do the things we want to do
    But our sole adventure today
Was to find a restaurant in Camorie!
    Somehow we are not disturbed,
Content to relax, sitting on the "veranda,"
    Enjoying the change of pace
And freedom in this new place.

Armin and I are happy to be together
    On vacation after the terrible trials
Of this past year.
    These times away
Have always been our happiest
    With relaxing, exploring
And enjoying each other.
    Now the possibility seems present
To have that same enjoyment all of the time
    In this new way of living.

Our vacation seems like a celebration
    Of good health, peacefulness within

And a new life evolving from our dreams.
    I like it!

It is impossible to comprehend
    How old everything is
In this land of Tuscany.
    My history is totally inadequate
To take in Etruscan and Roman times
    From my sheltered life in America
Where nothing man-made stands older
    Than two or three hundred years.

THE TUSCANY HOUSE, INSPIRED THE
PAINTING ON THE NEXT PAGE BY BILL

Vacation in Tuscany

We have spent two weeks with our friends
    In Tuscany.
It is very special to be together with them.
    Each year we make times to be together
In their home in Philadelphia
    Or ours in Rochester.
Lois and I have been friends for thirty-five years
    Ever since we took our children

On the adventure to work
    On the Apache Reservation,
That experience creating the beginning
    Of our friendship.

Lois and Bill were married the year I met Armin
    And now it is twenty years
For Armin and me.
    We consider it
One of our great good fortunes
    That our husbands, Armin and Bill,
Have also become good friends.
    We have had
Several vacation adventures
    But this is the longest time
We have spent together.

This year Bill wanted to see the art in Tuscany
    An extension of his study of art
At the Academy where he has spent
    The last three years as a student.
We rented the house in Tuscany
    That turned out to be
Up a winding narrow road into the mountains
    Above the village of Camorie.
That we survived two weeks of driving
    Up and down the road without incident,
We consider a great accomplishment
    Especially as Lois and I
Were the only ones we allowed to drive the car
    Up the hill.

We learned that coming home
     Late at night in the dark, while scary,
Was the best way
     To avoid meeting other cars on the road,
Since it seemed everyone else
     Was already eating and drinking
And enjoying themselves
     In the safety of their own homes.

In the beginning we shopped for food,
     Settled into our house,
Slept to rest from our travels, cooked and ate,
     Drinking wine, of course,
Except for Bill who drinks vodka.
     Armin began to search
For new Italian wines.
     It was a great adventure for him
Since before, he knew and liked
     Only French wines.
But we were the beneficiaries,
     Enjoying the wine and his enthusiasm.
The beautiful women at the wine store
     Added to his enjoyment!

We made many day trips to see Italy—
     Luca, Pisa's Leaning Tower,
The beautiful cathedral
     And open race track in Sienna
We saw the marble fields of Carrara
     Where the cutting is still going on
In the same places where it began

Two thousand years ago.
        And from where came the marble
For Michelangelo's magnificent creations.
        We were able to bring home pieces
Gathered at the edge of the quarry.

We went to the Opera to see
        Le Turandot as part of the Puccini Festival
Outside, under the stars and
        Beside a lake, a magnificent evening.
What a gorgeous way to experience opera,
        Something I have had little of.

We spent two days in Florence
        Packed with sight seeing of churches,
Museums of Italian art and sculpture.
        The highlight was Michelangelo's David
Which Armin had seen fifty two years ago,
        Not realizing it was a copy until later.

He was so overwhelmed to see the David
        He said he could go home then
A lifetime's dream fulfilled.

I have left behind my worries for these days.
        I had said I would be in touch
About my business affairs
        But with the isolation of our house
The cell phone, not working, I was free.
        Gradually I let it all go
To enjoy this time away and be with Armin

And our friends.

My mind remembered at first, the connection,
    With another of our vacations
With our friends.
    But I decided, slowly,
That the university would not intrude again.
    Surprisingly I have not worried
About what awaits me when I return.
    I will deal with it then.
I am on vacation now.

It is two years since Armin and I
    Have had a vacation like this
And these times away have been
    Some of our happiest together.
But this year is different.
    The cancer and all its upheaval
In our lives,
    The confrontations about our relationship
Have brought us to a new place
    And I feel happy and often peaceful.
I will not soon forget the meals we shared
    Sitting with Lois and Bill on the veranda.
Bill turned the wood fired oven for baking pizza
    Into a fireplace for our enjoyment
On the rainy cool August nights
    In our mountain retreat.

Across the mountainside we look out
    On a cluster of old homes

With gorgeous bougainvillea
    Covering one side.
We listen, with amazement,
    As carpenters work on the houses,
Playing magnificent opera music
    Which fills the valley
Resonating off the mountain walls,
    Filling the air with magical sounds.

Everything is old.
    It has been here a long time.
The changes made
    For modern convenience,
The barely widened road

245

To make room for a car
   To climb the mountain,
Are but small adjustments
   The land has allowed without changing
Its sense of timelessness.

All this has helped me to slow down,
   Let go of my usual world
And just be here.
   I say a prayer that all is well
In my family world while we are away.

I am grateful for this time of relaxation,
   Letting go of my cares and worries
Trying to manage everything.
   I have been on vacation in Tuscany
And now I am ready to be at home.

I am fulfilled by the beauty of it all!

Home Safely

We are home—safely,
    Despite my dream on the plane
That we were being attacked
    As we flew.
It was so real
    I could hardly believe it wasn't true.
Only Armin's saying,
    "I was awake and nothing changed,"
Made it clear that I had been asleep,
    Dreaming.

We had been more isolated and out of contact
    In our mountain retreat
Than I was really comfortable with.
    Even Lois's international cellphone
Did not work
    Until we were away from our house
And the mountains.
    Gradually I let go of my worry
And let myself have time to be away and relax.
    It was a wonderful time in so many ways.

But coming home is always stressful—
    Is the house all right? Did Junie do OK?
With his four visits a day from friends?
    I always hold my breath a bit
Until we are home and I see that the house is safe.
    And there Junie was, so glad to see us,
His tail wagging wildly.

My first anxious call was to Cindy.
    When I reached her, she was fine
And had just talked with Lisa and her dad
    So all was well.

The pile of mail and newspapers
    Is overwhelming
And this time important documents
    Are awaiting me.
I open the letter from Tom, my attorney,
    And see the draft agreement
From the university has arrived.
    I am too tired to take it further
And set it aside until I have slept.

Much is riding on this next step in my future
    And in our lives together.
If all goes well, I will sign the agreement
    Resigning through retirement—
In two years.
    I will have time to do my work,
To launch my new career.

It is very scary to cut loose from this past.
    With only myself and together with Armin
To chart our future.
    The security of income
And health insurance
    Have become big issues in facing aging,
Especially so with Armin's cancer
    And the damage to my retirement funds

Like so many others who had fared
        Much worse in the crash of the stock market.

I reach back into my past
        When only optimism and trust
Were all I had to chart my way
        With my own ingenuity and intellect.
My world has grown wider and richer
        Through decades of experience
Surely, I tell myself, *I can do as well now*
        As I was able to do then.

So I face the morning with hope and calm.
        It is our twentieth anniversary.
It has been a rough transition
        From this idyllic world we lived in
While we let the world go on without us
        And we were on vacation.

But we are talking about what is happening
        As we face this next step.
Armin has joined the other Bill
        To go exercise at the Y,
A tradition and habit of many years
        And we will begin to lose the weight
Of too much of everything.
        Andrea will pamper me today
With a facial and pedicure
        To repair the damage of sun
And the blisters on my feet

Which I managed to avoid
    Until the very last night
Of walking in Florence.

Kathy has done a yeoman's job
    Of watering my garden
Through two weeks of 90 degree weather
    Which only yesterday broke,
Just in time for our return.
    I would have been exhausted
Staying here, just trying to keep up
    With the garden in the heat.
Jeannine has cleaned the house
    So all is fresh upon our return.
I cleaned the refrigerator on the last day
    Knowing nothing would survive
The two and a half weeks away.
    So everything is a fresh start
In many ways, despite the fact
    I have only today
Before I must reenter the university world.

On the airplane, I finished Frances Mayes'
    Under the Tuscan Sun.
My fantasies of having a home in France
    Got a stronger dose of reality
Than I was prepared for or she intended.
    The home she made there in Tuscany
I have made here in our beautiful old home.

Going through all of that again
    Does not hold the lure it held for her.
For the moment I am content to be home—
    Safely—
To pick up the letter
    And begin to reconnect with our future
And my hopes and optimism
    For myself, once again.

It has been a healing journey in some way
    Another major step in my transition
To my New Life.

A Moment in Time

I want to acknowledge this moment in time
    Between the end of vacation
And the rest of my life.
    I will go today to the university
For the opening meeting
    But for me it is the first day
Of my new life.

I will have two years,
    To write and make my way
Into the next phase of my life's work.

I don't know what it will become
    What concrete evidence
Will document my efforts
    But I am very aware that the time is mine
A gift to use wisely or waste
    By not believing in myself.

I began my working life
    With a dream and hope and optimism
That I could make it happen.
    The confidence of youth was mine.
I have not done it all
    But step by step I have done a lot.
Dreams have been fulfilled
    And dreams have failed.
But the effort has been the same.

Step by step, by trusting in myself and the process,
        Refining the goal as needed.
I have kept my way.
        I will write about empowerment—
My own and the work I've done
        To help others find their own.
It will empower me to engage in the dream,
        Working to make it happen.

I have many skills today I did not have
        At earlier times.
Insight, maturity, realism, experience.
        Surely, if I could make it happen
When I was seventeen,
        I can do it again now.

One difference is the culture and beliefs
        That growing is for the young
And withdrawing and coasting for the old.
        I am at that magical marker
Of retirement.
        But I will not follow that path
To obsolescence.
        I will create my own path of aging
        "Older and Growing," as Carl wrote,
        About his own moment in time.
Shared dreams and space
        To quell the fears of living,
                I will overcome.
I will enjoy the not knowing
        That takes me into the future.

OUR HOME

256

Returning Home Firestorm

The first thing I saw when I opened the door
    Returning home at 10pm
From our time away
    Was the mountain of mail
And newspapers Kathy had left stacked
    In the hall, even adding a note
On the mirror above it,
    Mail ↓ with a downward arrow!

The message machine stood at 12
    And now ten days later still has
One unreturned message,
    Awaiting reaching the top
Of my priority list.
    We opened the mail
From attorneys that night,
    Finding the letter
With the university's response.
    I put it aside to read the next day
When I was rested.

My attempts to be orderly and self caring
    Have been like holding an umbrella
While standing outside in a torrential rain
    With the wind blowing hard.
I can't imagine how much worse it could be
    If I had not at least tried
        To take things one at a time.
By the time I got through the first week

Of the university, home, garden and life chaos,
        I took to my bed and stayed there
        Most of two days—
Conducting my business in bed
        While trying to regroup.

I had seen Chris the week before
        Listening to his experience
Of returning to work
        After a wonderfully restful vacation.
A firestorm he called it.
        Suddenly I have a word
That begins to name my experience
        Of these past ten days.

Everything I left behind in going away,
        I have to pick up the pieces in returning.
Some are good—
        The house did not burn down
Junie is OK and delighted to see us,
        Not the worse for his four daily visits
And a walk each day
        Which is more than he gets
When we are home.

My garden has been cared for by Milli
        While I was away.
Kathy struggled mightily to keep my flowers
        Alive in the 90 + degree heat
That continued every day,

Breaking only the day before
　　We returned home.
But the lack of water volume
　　Was a constant struggle.

Thomas is glad I am back,
　　Concerned for me in the firestorm
But soon we are laughing
　　At least for the moment
About the craziness of life.

I enjoyed Andrea's care of my feet and face
　　Which puts me in a state
Of deep relaxation.
　　Stephanie found a new hair appointment
Just one day after the one I had to cancel.
　　And Benjamin and Michael
Did their magic on my hair.

I picked blackberries with Jeanne
　　Freezing the huge black jewels
For jam and cobbler I will soon make.
　　I am grateful for these moments of peace
In this firestorm of returning home.

The news of the death of a colleague
　　After her fierce battle to live,
Creates an underlying stream of sadness
　　As I remember her admonition to me,

"Do what makes you happy.
    You never know
What is around the corner."
        —*Marg Sovie*

But something is different.
    The moment in time has also registered
In my consciousness.
    That I am entering a new phase of work
And another transition in my life.

The last four years
    Have been times of exploration
While standing still in my work.
    Drawing on long held skills of teaching
To be with students in their learning,
    Now I am beginning a new phase
Of writing about the work I have done.

Empowerment will soon consume
    Its central place in my work.
It is as if many of the plugs I reinsert
    Into the place it has held in my life
Do not quite fit.
    Something has changed.

I am overwhelmed by the volume on my plate.
    But I am irritable with the lack of fit.

I blew up at Armin and said,
> The water line has to be fixed NOW!
And by the way, the porch steps
> Have to be done as well.
They look a mess and we've put off
> Fixing them for two years.
Suddenly I am trying to confront
> The differences between us
In how we live in and care for our house.
> I see it all as part of the firestorm.
And Armin really does not like it
> When I lose it and yell at him!

* * * * * * * *

Postscript:
In Armin's desk I found a yellow sticky note:
"Why do you talk to me like this? I would never talk
to you that way." I have nothing to connect his note
with except that he did not like me to yell at him. I
am glad he could write how he felt but I so wish he
had been able to say that to me directly.

It was sad the lengths he would go to avoid conflict!

Craziness

We were talking in the group
    About mothers and their self-absorption,
And demanding ways, labeling them as crazy.
    One person asked what is craziness
And we didn't answer the question.
    I think, for me, craziness is being cut-off
Or separated from feelings,
    In myself or in others.

When I couldn't connect
    With my mother's feelings
I held myself aloof and separate
    Sensing it was not safe to go there
With her when I couldn't feel the connection
    Between us.
With my dad, it was different.
    I could always feel
The connection between us and sense
    His realness, even when it wasn't spoken
In words.

Talking about this in the group
    And feeling disconnected from some
Invaded my dreams in a nightmare of people.
    When I awakened and described it
As crazy, I knew what had triggered it.

Armin and I talked long in the night
    Going over what has happened

These last days and gradually I could connect
        My feelings and what they represented
In my life and in the life I have experienced
        With him.

It is better between us now.
        Things are different.
I can say what I want,
        Knowing that he will take my feelings
Seriously.
        I am still unsure about trusting this
But I am checking it out
        And validating that it is true.
I like this new reality between us
        Very much.
It is no longer crazy and confusing.

Finally I could sleep again.

The Pieces of the Puzzle

The pieces of the puzzle are coming together
    The best of the old and the new
Fitting together as if intended all along
    By some magic greater than myself.

I have opened myself to the universe
    Taking in new possibilities
Which caught my interest, generating energy
    And response—the delight of discovery
And the gift of new visions
    Slowly replacing my war-torn inner life.

The process has been
    Like a slowly meandering stream
Knowing where its path lay
    But moving forward in curves and falls,
Beautiful in its own time and place,
    While moving inexorably
On to a destination—
    Joining with other streams and voices
Into a river flowing toward the ocean.

This naturalness of the universe
    And my becoming one with it
Has been healing,
    Washing away the pain and loss
Leaving me refreshed
    With new vision
    And energy for my life and work.

I learned at many moments
    That I could not push the river
Or think my way through
    In goal setting or problem solving
As I had lived so much of my life before.

I could only trust the still small voice within
    Guiding me to the next step
With my response,
    Knowing it worked or didn't
Appearing often at night in my restless dreams
    Or the peaceful quiet of the morning sun.

It would be a mockery of truthfulness
    To say that what happened was good
Because it created this time.
    It is more honest to acknowledge
That I recognized the risk the volcano wrought
    Saw that my life was endangered
And took action to find my way out
    And through to a New Life for me.

I am grateful for the gifts of others
    Who have stayed with me
Through the terror
    And now say I am inspiration
For those changes that lie ahead for them.
    I did not hope to be that.
But in sharing my journey
    I hope to connect with others in theirs
And for them to know the hopefulness

That good can come
    Through crisis and tragedy.

In following my own path,
    And feeling the surprise and delight
In the journey and in where I travel
    As well as in where I land,
The pieces of the puzzle come together,
    showing their magnificent
Pattern for my life.

I see in images and beauty the gift of life
    And the gift of giving.
I see the possibility for sharing with others
    In love and connection and joy.

Sleepless, Nightmare Nights

They don't come as often
    As they did in the beginning—
These restless nights that leave me exhausted—
    Sometimes they are sleepless nights
With no awareness of why I am awake.
    Others are filled
With frightening nightmares
    Knowing I have done something wrong
And those I love are harmed.

I have learned that I am all the parts
    In these unfolding dreams of my dreams
I am the one to blame.
    I am the one hurt by the blame;
I am the one who acted;
    I am the one acted upon.

In all these dramas there is shame
    And embarrassment at what I have done
I am the one unworthy
    Who has brought about this shame.
I shame myself
    As others shame me
Leaving my heart pounding
    As the drama unfolds.
I am marked in this latest dream
    My head shaved in one place.
I am being sent away
    To Australia—where thieves

And murderers were sent from England
     In their earliest days of settlement
Sometimes for only stealing a loaf of bread.

I have an active imagination in those dreams
     A word or cross look can get it started
And in my dreams I am alone
     Unloved, unwanted.

Thank goodness we've moved beyond
     The days when people were beheaded,
Especially women,
     Who angered their husbands
In the days of England I am reading now.

I've learned to live with these sleepless nights
     And to survive the nightmare dreams.
A stack of books and light sit beside my bed,
     Available to see me through the night,
I simply play the parts until the drama is over
     As I face another day.

But writing has become my friend
     For recording these human dramas
Of mine.
     Sometimes poetry emerges
As I waken
     But always there are Morning Pages
To help me clear my mind
     And be ready for the day.

A bit shopworn by all the work and drama,
    I am still myself,
Knowing that I am progressing
    Through my sleepless, nightmare nights
To a new life of hope and promise.

Women's Lives

For many years I have read of women's lives
    And explored how they came to be
The person they were.
    What they were born with—
What life events—
    What choices and decisions
Got them to that place in life
    Where books were written
To tell their story.

I even taught my students
    About what I had learned.
In classes focused on their careers
    I helped them see first
Outside themselves
    Through other women's lives.
I hoped that they might gain
    A new perspective
About their own choices and decisions.

Composing a Life,
    Mary Catherine Bateson called it.
She shared not only her life
    As daughter of Margaret Mead
And Gregory Bateson,
    But those of friends
Willing to share their stories.

Now it seems prophetic
	That I prepared in some way
To delve within myself for this new challenge
	Of composing the next phase of my life.

As I begin to see my future rising
	In my continually working brain,
I see the pattern emerging
	Of telling the stories of others—
Both women and men perhaps—
	Through both my writing
And photographs.
	They are powerful mediums
Through which to see
	The stories of our lives—
Both theirs and mine.

Last Teaching

I spent three of the last five years
    Of my employment in the university
Teaching nursing courses.
    In my classes
I had both young students
    And RNs returning to school.

I taught the course on Family
    And had the best class ever
When I used the film, "StepMom"
    With Julia Roberts
And Susan Sarandon.
    The story contained all the elements
Of family affected by divorce, remarriage,
    Young children
And the impact of terminal illness
    In the mother.
I gave the students assignments
    In small groups
To pay attention to the elements in the story
    Before we watched the film.
They did a wonderful job
    In sharing with their classmates
The important aspects of how the family
    Was affected in the story.

They were thrilled by the class
    Which engaged their interest
Enthusiastic, acknowledging

(While implying their boredom
With so many classes—
Both mine and those of others).

What I learned was the power
    Of finding a medium
So close to their worlds of daily life—
    Films, TV engage them
As I had never considered before.

I also taught a course
    On Death, Loss, Transition,
While going through my own.
    I remember it was facilitative
In helping them see and acknowledge
    The losses in their lives,
Small and large.
    They had a lot of flexibility
To express their learning.
    One student made a poignant scrapbook
Of her experience of abortion
    That had occurred that semester.
Somehow, she left it with me at the end,
    The keeper of the loss
She did not want to take with her
    Or share with anyone else in her life.
I was touched to hold it for her—still.

One student took advantage of the freedom
    And did not fulfill her obligation
To learning.

I felt used and realized
    I had given away too much,
Not able to hold her accountable
    For her actions.
It was an important learning
    For me.

I remember another course,
    The final clinical integration for RNs
Completing their BS degree.
    It was a new level of competence
They were achieving in their practice.
    Their knowledge and seriousness
About their learning touched me
    In their growth.

It is interesting to me
    That I never wrote of any of this
In my transition.
    It is clear that in my inner world
I had already left it behind me
    Despite my care for the students.

Good-Bye

I have said good-bye to the university
    Though I am the only one who heard it.
As I neared the end
    Of the work I had undertaken.
Trying to bring completion,
    My impatience is almost overwhelming.
But finally, the work is done
    And the continuity handed to others.

I have a year remaining
    In the agreement with the university.
But my accountability is to the writing
    And my transition away from there
Because no one really cares what I do now—
    But me.

I have been working with others
    On the transition.
Jim is helping me with the equipment I need
    And the skills I must acquire
To do my own work on my computer.
    I had not ever done even my email,
Always having a secretary,
    For nineteen years!
Neal has told me about new video technology
    And is working with me to make usable
The films we made over the years.

At home, Gerry is building new bookcases
        So that I can fill them with the books
From my work—those I want to keep.
        By the fall the bookcases will be ready
And week by week, I will carry home books,
        Leaving empty shelves
        In the life I leave behind.
So it seems that all is orderly.

But in the past month
        My interior life has exploded in sadness.
It is as if all the feelings of loss I could not feel
        In those first months
Have now returned, unimpeded.
        They threaten to overwhelm me.

My trip to Kansas brought sadness unbounded
        As my sister and I
Traversed the fields of old—
        The cemetery to take the flowers
To mark the graves
        The Arboretum where all is in disarray
In the place we created
        As the Harlow Memorial Trees
And the arbor named for my mother.

I did not even look at the place
        Where our home once stood.
I did not need the added loss
        Of seeing the parking lot for the school.

We drove to see my aunt
      Who lives in the very small town
Where my mother spent her growing up years
      And left as a young woman
To make her place in the world.
      I was touched
By the openness of the hills
      But grieved that I knew so little about her
In ways I now can never know.

It is not a single loss I grieve
      As huge as it was to lose my work
And place in the world.
      It is a lifetime of losses
Finally all open
      And in reliving them,
I hope to find my Self
      Renewed, strengthened
And ready for my New Life.

New Life

I have been reconstructing my life
    For a long time.
Suddenly it seems to be in new ways.
    I began putting the records
Of my academic life on the wall in my studio,
    As if reclaiming my past.

I began writing for our center website
    Focusing on the areas of work I know
Attempting to define what I want to do.
    Soon I will have to think about marketing
Telling others who might use my services.
    But for now this is a start.

My photography website is a source of joy,
    My own creation,
As much as the photographs
    Shared in my gallery
Waiting for connections with others
    Who might find beauty in them
And buy them for their own.

All this time I have been slowly moving
    The accumulated books and papers
To find their places in my life and home.
    Suddenly the time is short
And the boxes fill my car,
    Trip after trip.

One day I spent in sadness
    Reminded of all that is not coming back.
But now I drive through old places
    That made a piece of my life
And say good-bye fondly.

I sent the email to friends
    Also in transition
Claiming a piece of work for my future
    And opened myself to the universe
And its flow.

I think of the things I want to do
    In bringing end
And closure to this venture
    That covered twenty-two years of my life.
They are acts of meaning,
    Of courage to embrace the end.
I am ready for this to end.
    It is time to move on.
I have already moved on
    To my new life.

Freedom

The last box has been carried home.
　　The place that was my office
Has nothing in it now
　　That would be identified with me.
I took the sign off the door
　　Announcing office hours I no longer hold.
I put a message on the telephone
　　So that if someone is looking for me
They can find me at home.
　　Soon they will disconnect the line
And it will be as if
　　I were never there.

I turned in the keys.
　　It is a small wrench
That I no longer have access to the building.
　　Of course, I do, during normal hours
And I may come a few more times
　　For the audio-visual work next door
To complete projects I still want to finish.
　　But I have no role here
And no need for keys.

I saw the one person
　　I once worked most closely with.
Our connection brought tears
　　To both of us.
It was a reminder of the respect
　　And love we shared

As we worked together day after day
      For so many years.

Now I am home completely
      And face the task
Of truly making a life for myself.
      One day I felt very sad
That I have no role or structure to guide me
      Or to create an identity.
But now I feel the freedom
      Of setting my own agenda.

My garden is the first focus and beneficiary
      Of my freedom.
I am actually enjoying my days
      And begin to feel the energy and joy
Of freedom.

* * * * * * * * *

April, 2013
I returned to the university for the only thing that
would bring me back—the retirement of Joanne.
Our connection is intact and I enjoyed seeing
her family of children and grandchildren there to
celebrate with her.
I went one last time to the PamAm Memorial for the
students who died to say good-bye to the university
and the world I once knew.
I will not return.

2015

I returned once more, to see Joanne at home, very ill with cancer that was taking her life. There was comfort for both of us in that time we shared, acknowledging the bond that remained. I was grateful to Vennie who told me in time so that I could go. I created a photograph in her memory— and took the notecards to the calling hours for her family—the source of Joanne's pride and of her joy —there to care for her at home to the end.

Letting Go

Emotion runs deep as the tide changes.
  I let go of a deeply held attempt
To shape my world,
  Giving in to the inevitable
That my view was not shared by the other.

It was an option to stay
  But I would have to accept
The shaping of my work by others.
  Tenure gave me that right.

I long ago realized that I do not respect
  The mission of the institution
Or the people leading it.
  All I could influence was my own decision
Not to contribute my talents
  To something I do not respect.

As I began the process of letting go,
  Negotiating an agreement
That would support my transition
  To a different future,
I let go of all the trappings
  That defined me as a university professor.
Letting go of the role, the identity, the work,
  Even my access to students
Whom I loved, but no longer want to serve.

All of those places inside of me
    That held the status, the identity
The security,
    I am letting them move into my past.

Cut Loose

The last tie to my old world ended,
    Balancing equipment I bought
Through the university.
    My last paycheck was $0.00!
I didn't realize how prophetic a sign it was.

When I was fourteen,
    In the aftermath of my sister's death,
I negotiated a job with my mother.
    I would help with the meals,
The housework and my siblings
    If grandmother did not return
To live with us.
    She agreed to pay me five dollars a week.

I spent my first pay
    On a down payment for a swimsuit
And charged the balance.
    The store, I am sure, consulted my mother,
But it was a small town
    And we were known.

My relationship with work, money and spending
    Was sealed in those transactions.
For fifty-three years it propelled me through life
    Always finding the next step
On a career ladder
    That included work I loved
    For many of those years.

In the beginning
     The future was filled with excitement
As I took each step through work
     And education
To meet my dreams.

Though I grew bored at various times
     I was always able to find another venue
Where my increasing skills and knowledge
     Could be exchanged for money,
Creating security and resources
     For my continually reinvented
Appetite for spending.

Now, by my own choice, I have severed the tie
     And cut myself loose. But—
I feel lost and confused in this first aftermath.
     I have done my homework
And have many options awaiting.

I even know that I am avoiding the work
     That would move me forward.
But there is some kind of clarity
     I am searching for,
Some connection to who I am
     That I need to guide me through.

I feel lonely as well
     As if I am the only one
Experiencing such confusion
     But Thomas reminds me

We are in the same boat
	Even though the waters we are rowing
Are different.

I have spent a month cleaning my garden
	From the aftermath of winter
And the abundance of spring.
	I think I will make one more round
Of the nurseries, looking for plants
	To liven the borders of my front garden.

I am stimulated by new pictures
	From the garden magazine
And the creativity of others.

The next steps back
	Are sitting on my desk
As papers and decisions
	To fund my own path—
And give time to let my work emerge..

I am cut loose, at last,
	From the tight connection
Of work rendered for a paycheck.

Cut loose.
	Letting go.
		Freedom dances inside my head.
Panic, resignation and hope
	Play out the sounds

That signal my place in life is over—
    Or just is being redefined.
Instead of one loss, I begin to feel
    The loss of wasted time
And wonder why it took me so long
    To recognize these powerful forces
Inside of me.
    I feel humbled by my riches
Of love and feelings and images of beauty
    And the opportunities before me.

Shell or Structure

Some days I feel the empty space inside
    As if there will never be anything there
Like meaningful work.

Other days it feels like structure
    I am building that will support my work.
First, I built the unused attic space
    Into a beautiful studio
And was excited that I had a place
    For all my creative work.
Yet other events intervened
    And little happened.

Now it is a serious time of transition
    Away from the university
Whose structure and demands
    Have guided and supported my work
For thirty-five years.

Gerry built the bookcases for my sitting room
    Which are now filled with floor to ceiling
Books from my office.
    They are visible holders
Of the world I lived in—
    The world of ideas.

The books play a new role of depository
    For the ideas of others
Upon whose work my own will rest.

My new equipment arrives today—
    The end result of countless hours
Of examination, questioning, dialogue with Jim,
    Will this do
What I need to support my work?
    Independently, away from
And separate from the university.
    The world of technology—
Printing, scanning, faxing, copying—
    In black and white and color
Will soon be driven by my new computer
    With software
That does all kinds of magic—
    If I can learn to use it!

My garden is once again the center
    Of my attention,
Putting down the mulch to hold the moisture,
    Smooth, even, connected, flowing—
Milli is again working on a new space
    Extending my garden in the back.
I am anxious about the change—
    Will it be beautiful, pleasing, restful
We will soon know.

I have chosen old rhododendrons
    From a nursery
Growing almost wild for many years.
    The plants are beautiful
And bring stability and timelessness
    To this new garden design.

Even my house is seeing changes—
	The steps have finally been replaced,
The porch is next with all new wood.
	The ugly makeshift vestibule
Which Armin built from old storm windows
	To keep out the cold
(And generating so many complaints
	From friends)
Is finally gone.
	And there is a beautiful new door
With changing glass and screen
	To accommodate the seasons.

The time is coming.
	The moment of truth—
Will I sit down and write?

I know I have things to say.
	But will I actually do it—
Or remain a shell.

The question haunts my sleep.
	The dark night is my soul.
But as I turn off the lamp
	I see the light beginning in the morning sky.
The trees stand in their usual place
	In my window.

Perhaps.

Rewriting

Rewriting, my writing friend, Jeanne, called it
    When I tried to skip over that part
By saying I was editing.

Did I somehow know
    It would be so painful
And such hard work
    To go back to the beginning
And relive it all over again?

It is not as raw as the first time through.
    The edge has faded
And blurred into my unconscious
    But the words bring it back
And I am exhausted by the effort
    Of remembering—and holding it back.

Yet I persist,
    Hopeful in my belief
That this may be of value
    To someone, somewhere
Confronting their own loss and grief—
    And encouraged to write their own words,
As I have written mine,
    I hope they find healing and relief
From their pain.

Looking Back

Each day is only one small step
     Following another.
My vision is distorted
     By the blinders around my eyes
Closing off both past and future
     So that I can find
The next step in front of me.

But when I stop and turn around,
     Looking back,
I can see where I began
     And know how far I've come.

I can spend a day painting
     With nothing else
Distracting my awareness,
     My mind and body totally engrossed
In creating on the canvas
     Some sense of my experience—
Often hidden from my conscious mind
     Until I see it in front of me.

Other days I write my Morning Pages
     Clearing my mind from the dregs of sleep.
Suddenly a poem appears
     As if full blown just waiting
For my pen to write it down.

At first each day was only
   A way to make it through
And not stand still
   Despite the fact I hadn't a clue
Where I was moving to.

But when I stop and turn
   I see the path I've walked
And some of the bread crumb markers
   Are still lying there
Like Hansel and Gretel left
   To find their way back home again
From their gathering food in the forest.

My walk can only go forward
   There is no going back—
No place to retreat or rest
   Only moving on to create
A new life for myself.

But I am still encouraged
   When I can look back
      And see how far I've come.

Night Flight

It is Christmas.
    Armin and I are in Oregon
With Lisa and Chris, Katie and Jacob.

Cindy's baby is due the first week in January.
    But we decided to take the risk
And went to Oregon to spend Christmas.

We had been to the beautiful park
    With small railroad cars
That carried us through the holiday decorations.
    It was a magical evening.

When we arrived home to Lisa's
    There was a message from Cindy.
She was in labor, going to the hospital!

My efficient daughter, Lisa,
    Midwife that she has been for so many years
Was on the phone booking tickets
    Before I even finished packing.
And off to the airport she took us
    For a 3am flight!

We flew from Portland to New York City,
    Got a taxi to take us to the hospital
And arrived just three hours
    After the baby was born—

Who eventually was named
Caitrin!
Mother and Father and baby doing well.
I was so excited!

Mairead was three,
Dressed in her turquoise velvet pant suit
She came to meet her new baby sister—
Along with her Grandmother
And Grandfather Hunter
And Aunt Sharon.
What a welcoming committee.

I remember Mairead,
Walking with her Dad to the car.
She looked a bit lost!

Armin went to Jerry's house.
I stayed with Cindy and the baby
As I had done before
When Mairead was born.

December 29th, 2005.
Welcome to the world, Caitrin
And to our Family!

Who knew what a special person
You would soon be!

* * * * * * * *

Postscript:
My favorite memory of Caitrin—
    That special person emerging
Happened on her birthdays.

For Caitrin's first birthday
    We all were together in Rochester
For Christmas—
    Lisa and Chris, Katie and Jacob
Cindy, Mairead and Caitrin
    And Armin and me.

I ordered an ice cream cake
    Decorated just for her
And had it in the freezer
    In the basement
(The access to which is through
a door in the dining room floor).

When we were ready for it,
    I brought up the cake,
Put the candles on it
    Lit them
And we sang to her.
    All special but not unusual.

The unusual part was the next year—

Same scene, celebrating
    Caitrin's second birthday
    With a special dinner
And suddenly she said,
    "Granny, you have to get the cake"
And pointed to the door in the floor!

She remembered for a whole year
    From 1 to 2!
    The cake was in the basement
Through the door in the floor!
    Smart kid!
Remembers what is important to her!

Another New Year

It is another New Year
    And I've begun
To reread <u>Simple Abundance</u>
    And added <u>Something More</u>.
I can tell I am in a new place
    More deeply open and grateful
For the riches of my Life.

Some of the riches are new
    Like the new peacefulness
With Armin
    But many have been there all along,
It is only I who has changed,
    Feeling more open
Able to take in the riches of the life
    I have created over these many years.

I remember the days of angst
    When I was younger
Feeling the secrets of life
    Were passing me by,
Leaving me unfulfilled and unhappy.

But I do not feel that way now.
    Even in the aftermath of terrible losses
I am discovering the joys and riches
    Of the life I live after so much striving.
I have explored so many pathways

In this open time
    And suddenly I realize
    I have many new balls to juggle
As my interests and inquiring passions
    Have opened new ways of life
For me.

It will take years
    To explore and develop
The creative projects I now am fascinated by.
    Time and resources must be allocated
In some sense of priority
    In order to pursue them all.
But I stand at the threshold of open doors
    Knowing it is my choice to walk across
Into new worlds for me.

World of writing I am in,
    Photography I am learning
I see the portraits in my mind
    Of the people's stories I want to tell.

I have discovered the release and joy
    Of paint and color
Spread on canvases in abstract forms
    That allow me to say without words
The feelings I experience
    And feel drawn to express.

It is only after the paint is dry
    That I sometimes see

What it was I was experiencing and then creating.
　　From a hidden part of me.

I remember the excitement of Provence
　　Finding the light in all kinds of ways
And places where we traveled—
　　My camera and I—
And I want more!
　　I feel the pull of far away
Of new places to explore
　　And old lighthouses to see again
And try to capture the fading light
　　In the sky of midnight blue.

My connections with Armin have deepened
　　Over this time.
I feel more peaceful
　　Especially when I can escape
To my beautiful studio
　　And work in quiet aloneness.

I am touched by many in this new life.
　　As I am open and share
The gift of myself and travels with them,
　　Their gifts return a hundredfold.

There are threats to this life
　　With Armin's health
And perhaps even of my own,
　　But joy is there
In this unfolding of Life

Drawn from a lifetime of adventure
And love.

Sometimes I hardly recognize
This person I have become
So different in the life I lead
From the one in that world I lost.

But in other ways
I feel like an old soul
Finally home
Joining with that childhood look
Of knowing who I am—
And actually liking me.

Two years ago I wrote
I want to find the calm center of my Self
The place where joy and love and light
Flow freely.
It feels as if I have.
And can bring it into my life
When I choose
If I am quiet and pay attention
To my Self.

A Timeless Moment

On the very edge between awake and asleep
    I saw the moon
Through the blue stained glass
    Hanging in our window.
The light of the moon illuminated the glass
    With a soft beautiful glow.

Such beauty stirs me to capture it
    But I was too close to sleep
To get my camera.
    I simply enjoyed it
Letting the glow enter my body
    Creating a wonderful sleep.

Later, sitting in my bed,
I watched the moon
Move into position
And got my camera!

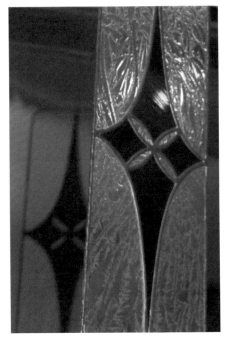

Love and Joy and Dreams

I want to live each day and moment fully
    With Joy
That my life will have been lived purposefully
    In the fullness of the gifts I was given.
That when it is over,
    I can let it go
With few regrets for missed opportunities.

I have used this time to confront my fears—
    To address the unaddressed—
To name the unnamed.
    I have explored new vistas
To create avenues of self-expression.
    The years have been productive
But not in a typically recognized way
    And sometimes not even clear to myself
Where I was going
    Or even if I was moving.

Now it is time to move ahead
    To continue making my world orderly
For a new life
    To extend my work into a new vision
And allow it to evolve in its own way.
    I must let go of ordering myself so tightly
And judging my efforts by lists completed.

This attitude adjustment will not come easily
     After years living in the old.
But I will try to live with awareness
     And create space and room
Inside myself
     For love and joy and dreams.

What Lay Ahead

I did not know what lay ahead
    When I wrote the conclusion
Love and Joy and Dreams
    With such optimism.

I had written my way
    Through Armin's prostate cancer
The fear unbounded for both of us—
    The impact on our lives—substantial.
But we recovered momentum
    And learned to live with it,
The chronic, but treatable condition
    As it became.

I was moving forward
    Auditing doctoral nursing courses
And reading and reading about empowerment
    Formulating my own concept—
While Armin began to have difficulty
    With his memory.
My practice was growing
    But the reality became clear—
I needed to focus
    To move my practice forward.

A lot happened in those years
    Between—

As you will see in Kaleidoscope!

Recently, I asked my friends for help
     In seeing my practice more clearly.
In an email dialogue,
     Chris said the impact was like a prism
     And wrote the poem,
     Prism Break.
Rebecca,
Responding to his image of the prism
     Said, "Like a kaleidoscope!"

The image is so powerful of what happens
     When people engage in psychotherapy
With me,
     I began to see it as a vision,
Wrote the poem
     And the title of my book was born.

Prism Break

I love the way the meadow grasses
     sooth the bottoms of my feet,
and brushing 'cross the tops of trees
     in wishful thought imaginings
is something close to ecstasy—

But not until I learn the way
     to loose the prism from my eyes
will I let go of what I've done
     and see the piddling splash it makes
in oceans far below—

Without the weight I lift my hands
     to touch the light of stars
and spread my arms beyond new worlds

G Christopher Basher
2016

Kaleidoscope

I stepped on a landmine
    And knew as I moved
        That the life I had known in my work
        Was over—
Blown apart in a million pieces.

My garden will be beautiful in the spring,
    I had said,
        And so will my life
Was the image that moved me forward
    Away from devastation.

It was Armin who was there for me
    Hurting in the use and betrayal of both of us.
By the time I arrived home
    He had found Tom Smith,
An attorney of great skill and tact
    And high regard.
His kindness made it possible to tell my story.
    It was his voice that stopped the attack
That would have made public
    The blame they laid on me—
Without acknowledgment of their own culpability.

Five years, before, my Father had died
    And I gave the eulogy to honor him.
I wrote my first poem,
    "What Have We Done To Him?"

To express my dismay about his medical care,
       The decisions made without real regard
       For the outcome.
My awareness of advance directives
       Became deeply real in those eight weeks
At the end of his life.

Just a month before the landmine, my mother died.
       In the twenty-two days we cared for her,
       From diagnosis of the cancer
       That took her life.
My feelings that the end of life
       Is a personal family matter
Became evident to me.

Again, I gave the eulogy and wrote it as a poem.

My personal voice—
       Both spoken and written
Was born in those events
       That altered my life.

In the aftermath of the landmine,
       I went to talk with Jim each week
To help me leave behind the loss and anguish.

Imbedded in those days as they emerged
       Was a freedom I had never known
Since my first employment
       At fourteen.
I was hurting so much from the attacks

I trusted no one but Armin
    (and Tom and Jim).
I joined Armin's group as a place to connect

And, soon, became co-therapist with Armin.

I found Julia Cameron's book, <u>The Artist's Way</u>
    And began to write Morning Pages,
Giving space to clear the chaos in my mind
    I awakened with each day.

I listened to the small voice inside,
    I wonder if I would enjoy painting,
And signed up for my first class.
    The unfinished canvas was not hopeful
But I signed up for another
    And my new voice was born.

I went for two weeks
    To the Maine Photographic Workshop
To advance my skill in a medium
    I had enjoyed for years during vacations—
Making beautiful photographs
    Of light and color and of my garden.

I wrote my way though all the pain
    In words and feelings,
Death, Loss, Transition, Change
    That matched the title of a course I taught
    When I returned to teaching.
It was many years before I could release

The words and images that flowed
From within my soul—
Letting them out in the open
For others to see and hear
In my beautiful books of poetry,
With my paintings and photographs.

I began the legal work to establish the Center
Armin and I had dreamed of
All those years before in the courtyard of the
Cathedral in Norwich, England,
The second year we were together.
We had made a placemark in stationery and napkins
But now it had a new name,
The Center for Human Encouragement.

The love and connection we share grew
In our daily life
In our work
In our family of two with our dogs,
Francie and Junie
With our children, Shakati, Meg, John,
Lisa and Cindy, and eventually, Thomas
And with the delightful grandchildren they gave us
Molly, Michael, Katie, Janie, Bobby, Jacob
Mairead, Caitrin—and Maeve
After Armin was gone—
The only sadness
That they would not know each other.

There were adventures of joy we created

In those days of freedom—
    Sailing on the coast of Maine—
Traveling with our friends, Lois and Bill
    On the canal in Provence
And a visit to Carcassone,
    Fulfilling Armin's childhood story
    Of its majesty.
And a house atop a mountain in Tuscany
    Where the carpenters' opera music
    Filled the air.
We visited Florence
    Where Armin sat fulfilled, beneath
    The magnificent statue of
    David.
Our vacation times were exquisite,
    Away from work,
We relaxed as our world grew
    In friendships and
In our person-centered world,
    In the special places we visited
    In Provence
    In Nantucket
    In Monhegan
    Sailing off the coast of Maine.

Perhaps the most delightful,
    The houses we rented alone in Provence
In Caromb, the first
    And the adventures from there
Along with my painting

And relaxing fulfillment of being together.

Despite the struggles in our relationship
    We were very happy together,
    The joy of connection and love
    The tenderness we gave each other
    Remained, in our way of being
        Together.
And then finally the tension was gone
    As well.

As I read again that Shakespeare sonnet
    Murray recited
    "Love is not love which alters
When alteration finds," lay just ahead.

Armin had been a therapist in Rochester
    For decades.
His reputation established,
    The clients continued to come
Despite the intrusive changes
    From insurance.
Finally he said, "I am semi-retired.
    But new ones found him
    On Psychology Today
(The only advertising he ever consented to).
    And he continued his work.

And then it all began to change.
    "How much can you earn?" Gerald asked,

When first I went to talk with him
    About our finances
In the unraveling of Armin's mind
    As the dementia began its inevitable decline.
I made a mental answer
    And put myself on Psychology Today,
My practice as a psychotherapist, now serious to me.

My work with clients grew and deepened
    As I listened and let in the pain in their lives
    And felt and saw the shifts
In perspective of the prisms that held them.

In Armin's decline, his clients became ours,
    Save two, who stayed alone with him
    Until the last week.

Our Center for Human Encouragement grew,
    A place of warmth and healing.
The depth of our connection with our clients
    Evident
    In the support and care they gave
        As Armin's body and voice declined—
Leaving him with the warmth of his eyes
    And his smile and sometimes short words
        To connect.

I cared for Armin at home, as I intended,
    Grateful beyond measure
        For Peter and others
Who helped to make it possible.
In all of it, I was all he needed.

In the aftermath, my wishes and determination
To be in charge in the ending of my life
Became as clear as the moon
In a beautiful night sky.
I will choose when I have had enough.

My journey through grief and loss has been unique
The many strands of our life wound together
In the love and connection we shared.

As the sadness moved out to sea,
I am surprised to feel
How much Armin's presence remains with me—
His love, respect, encouragement there—
As it always was.

It has sometimes been disconcerting
As I work to finish this book
That I am reliving many of those earlier feelings
In this new transition
After the death of Armin.

But from those days of loss and transition
Both old and newer,
My world is changing, once again,
I still turn on the lights.

My garden is beautiful—
In the spring
And in the summer
And in the fall.

The lights in my back garden are beautiful at night,
Especially in the winter.

And so is my life, beautiful.
I am grateful in many ways for all that I had.
And for what remains
In my home,
In my work
And in friends and family.
Armin's presence remains in my life
The memories of our life
The home we created. It often feels
As if he is still in the library
Once his, with special mementos
From his clients,
Is now mine with clients
With some of my own special mementos!

My clients hold special meaning
As I hear their stories
And am present with them
As their work moves them to healing.
It provides a sense of purpose in my life.

My own loss moves further away
In the riches of the life I had—and have.

Junie Too came to live with me on New Year's Eve
A tiny yellow lab puppy
Fulfilling my dream when Junie died.

Too young to leave his litter,
      He hadn't learned not to bite—
My hands and arms the evidence
      That I was his target!

Sleeping in his crate beside my bed
      Was the only peaceful time we had.
His barks took me out in winter
      To an often moonlit sky,
The light of my backyard garden so beautiful
      I almost forgot it was 3 am.
I carried him up and down the stairs,
      Scared as he was by them,
Until he was too big for me to carry
      And he moved to the big crate in the kitchen.

I signed up for training classes
      The same night I went to the pet store
To get food and toys and a crate for him!
      But he grew so rapidly
And was so strong,
      I took him to Tim, the trainer,
At only four months old
      Despite our weekly classes.
Tim's comment was validating,
      "Junie has a mind of his own,"
Tim was able to work wonders with Junie
      But I still struggled—

How to convince him I am in charge
      When he is much stronger than me!

Our old friend, Dr. Paul Black,
        Was very encouraging
That he is a handsome yellow lab puppy
        And will be fine—
As I learn to train him!

I am grateful for Junie's company.
        Our friend Vu,
Discovered Junie's favorite game—
        Kicking or throwing his ball
For Junie to chase
        Returning it to go again.
He loves it and we can only stop
        When we come in and put the ball
                In the cupboard!
Even so, he learns new tricks to keep it going!
But as soon as either of us goes into the kitchen,
        He goes to show us where the ball is
"Can we go to play now?"

In the summer heat
        He gets his exercise and is panting so hard
He is mostly ready to stop after just a few minutes.
        But very shortly with a big drink of water,
He is ready to go again!

His game of ball has been destructive
        To parts of my backyard garden.
I will have to see what survives the winter
        And how to make it possible
For my garden and Junie to co-exist!

JUNIE TOO

In spite of that, I am grateful for his company.
    I enjoy him and hope he will become
A well-behaved dog
    To greet our guests.
I want him to sit beside me in the library
    And even to sit with clients
        When he can be quiet.

Our wonderful grandchildren grew—
    Each becoming their unique being.
With challenges of their own
    They grow in the love and support
Of their families—
    Providing delight.

I have begun dance classes,
    Finally attending to my body,
Fulfilling the sign I got from Thomas,
    "I Hope You Dance!"

The completion of this book.
    Will mark the opening of new doors
Unknown, but challenging,
    And hopeful.
Kaleidoscope:
    My Changing World!

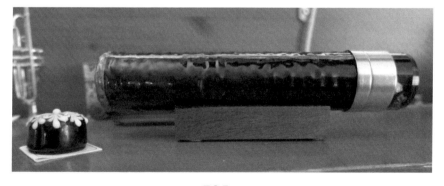

About the Author

GRACE HARLOW KLEIN
Photo credit:
Michelle Macirella
Luminaria Photography

Grace Harlow Klein
is a psychotherapist in
the Center for Human
Encouragement, the
dream she shared with her
beloved husband, Armin.
She continues to write
poetry, paint and take
photographs, making her
special books, sharing
her world of beauty,
experience, love,
feelings, awareness,
connection and insight.

She invites your response
to Kaleidoscope: My Changing World.

www.graceharlowklein.com
www.centerforhumanencouragement.com
www.graceharlowfineart.com

Grace@graceharlowklein.com

326

ARMIN IN VENASQUE, PROVENCE

CENTER FOR HUMAN ENCOURAGEMENT
ROCHESTER, NY

327